ACTING IN CHICAGO

How to Break Into Theatre, Film & Television

By

Belinda Bremner

Chicago Plays Inc.
2632 N. Lincoln
Chicago, IL 60614
312.348.4658

For Ben and Lucy, of course.

Do whatever you dream.

And with grateful thanks to
Yolanda Lyon Miller, Ted Hoerl and Rick Levine.

For information address Chicago Plays Inc., 2632 N. Lincoln, Chicago, IL 60614, (312) 348-4658.
ISBN: 1-56850-038-6

Contents

PREFACE

Talent is not enough. Neither are timing, luck, looks or networking. What you need to be a successful, professional actor in Chicago or any city is a generous helping of all these factors. But that is not enough either. You need to know the rules and keep to them. Behave as a professional and you can be considered a professional.

You may be lucky enough to graduate from a college that offers a course that explains the business of acting. You may find a class offered by a training center. You may have the great good fortune to have a mentor or fairy godmother. But don't count on it. And don't count on your agent to have the time to explain it all to you.

There is a cliché that "You never get a second chance to make a first impression." Trite and tired, but like most clichés, true.

Please note that the use of the feminine gender when referring to agents and casting directors is for simplicity. There are many fine male agents and casting directors in the Chicago area.

Belinda Bremner

PART ONE:

HOW THE BUSINESS WORKS

TALENT AGENTS

Why do I need an agent?

An actor in Chicago needs a union franchised agent (signatories for the Screen Actor's Guild, Actor's Equity, etc.) to get union work. This includes principal work in films and television, commercials, film industrials and voice-over. Principal means work above the level of extra. Some agents also handle print work (photographic modeling for advertisements or catalogues) and live industrials (trade shows in which actors are used to demonstrate and explain products). Agents may be asked by casting directors to book (hire) the extras for a union commercial. Some agents will arrange auditions for Equity productions and negotiate theatrical contracts.

There are non-union agencies as well. These represent non-union actors or actors who belong to one but not all of the three unions (AEA, SAG, AFTRA). Their clients are non-union, non-signatory companies and directors. Through them the beginning actor can book work which will give him or her valuable experience. Be warned though that, through no fault of the agent, there is no union here to protect you. The pay can be considerably lower than union minimum and there have been cases of producers who have not lived up to their contractual agreements.

Non-union actors CAN get work through union agencies, thus bringing them closer to union membership. (See the chapter on unions.)

How do you find an agent?

This is an important question with no single, simple answer. Finding the right agent is a vitally important part of becoming successful. Your agent must share your vision. You must believe in and respect one another. It must be a partnership. Choosing an agent is like choosing a doctor, a roommate, a mate. But how?

Local agents are listed in the Act One Reports, a pocket sized directory listing agents, casting directors, theatres and all the general information an actor needs. It is updated at least twice a year to keep up with the comings and goings of the personnel at agencies and theatres (they can be a fairly nomadic lot).

In the Act One Reports agencies will state their policies regarding representation and registration, union affiliations and areas of concentration. Some agencies offer "exclusive" representation. This means you are represented by this agency only. Many agencies will allow you to be "multi-listed," either across the board, or for particular areas of work (i.e. industrials or voice-overs). A discussion of "exclusive" versus "multi" listing follows. Some agencies will allow you to apply for representation in person. Many will only consider submissions by mail. There are agencies which only book non-union work. There are some agencies which concentrate their representation on specific ethnic groups. The staff of each agency is also listed, identifying who at each agency handles film or print or children.

Look through the listings. Ask around about the various offices. A warning here: some actors will have horror stories, real or invented, about agencies. Don't believe everything you hear from one or two people. Go for a consensus. Decide in which agencies you are interested. Then try to get in to see them.

Why is it so hard to get an agent's attention?

It is good to remember as you enter this sometimes baffling, often frustrating world of agents that you are only one of a multitude with the same intention. Some, like you, have trained, have done their homework, have real talent and discipline. Some, on the other hand, have only dreams and fanciful notions of instant fame and fortune. They have been exploited by "charm schools" and bogus acting teachers to whom they have paid large fees to be fed lies about their talent and potential. Some have totally unrealistic perceptions of themselves and what is required to make a life in this business. Some are just playing at acting. Some are certifiably insane.

Whatever their sort and condition, they believe they want "in." More often than not they will call an agent directly and ask "How do I become a movie star? How do I make it big? How do I get my own television show?"

Agents and their beleaguered receptionists field calls like this hourly. It is time-consuming for them but it also complicates your job. Because of these people, agents have had to set up protocols and isolating procedures to protect their time. It complicates and frustrates the serious actor. But take comfort in the fact that it allows the agent to spend more of her time negotiating serious work for serious actors like you.

The best way to secure representation is to have the agent approach you. That way there is the perception she is persuing you, not you her. This can happen if the agent sees you in a play, film or showcase. She will ask you to come to the office to talk. So, if you are in a play (any play) or showcase, be sure to send mailings to all the agencies and casting directors asking them to come. Be sure you include a way in which they can reach you.

Of course, the easiest way to get an agent's attention is to know someone on the staff. That doesn't happen all that often.

Another option is to ask a friend or teacher who is represented by the agency if he or she can get you an appointment or if you can use their name in requesting one. Some may be reluctant to do this, but Chicago is a very friendly city and many in the business are more than happy to help a newcomer- especially if they believe in your talent. Be aware that just because a particular agent is good for your friend or teacher, she may not be the right agent for you.

Most agencies have a policy that prospective talent must first mail in a picture and resume before they will even consider granting an appointment. Based on the picture and resume, they will decide if they will see you. A cover letter, short and professional, should accompany the picture and resume. Generally allow several weeks for the agency to plow through the mountains of submissions they receive daily. They will get back to you as soon as they can. Calling daily to check on the progress of your submission is a really nonproductive way to begin a relationship. Send off the packets and spend the waiting time insuring that you are really ready to see them when they do call.

Some agencies will allow you to drop in personally to register.

What will I need to show or tell an agent?

Show up at an agency with professional headshots (pictures), resumes, a couple of monologues to perform if called for and a good book. You may have to sit a while.

Pictures are essential in getting work. Getting what all concerned consider the right picture can be a nightmare. Agents, even within the same agency, may not agree on who is the best photographer and which of the shots on your proof sheet are the most marketable. This can be maddening because you want to please everyone and, probably, have limited financial resources. But you need good pictures. Never scrimp here. Cheap pictures look like cheap pictures.

A professional-looking resume is also essential and along with pictures discussed in detail later (see Tools of the Trade). But for now know that no matter how little experience you have, you need a resume. And that resume should be cut to 8x10 inches and affixed to your professionally developed picture.

The monologues should be geared for film or television. Great big, dramatic pieces which fill a theatrical stage are inappropriate for this. Remember you will probably be performing these across the desk from the agent. Choose smaller pieces and work on them with a coach. Have a variety of monologues ready- comic, serious. Choose only pieces which fit your age and type: for film you will rarely be asked to play any older than you look naturally. Avoid dialects. And many agents say they are truly weary of pieces which bash either sex or recount in graphic detail a first sexual encounter.

The choice of book you bring to the audition, its subject matter, length and jacket design are entirely up to you. Its sole purpose is to entertain you while you wait.

How should I behave?

Be polite, and do not monopolize time. You may think you are being given short shrift or treated coldly. That may be true or it may be your perception because of nerves. Whatever the case, answer the behavior with politeness. There is no excuse for rudeness on anyone's part but that doesn't mean it doesn't happen in this high pressure, high-risk, low-paying business. Remember all the time wasters who are calling the agents. It may be a particularly bad day. Give the frantic receptionist another chance. Allow that the agent may just have lost a negotiation or a client. If you sign with the agency and this behavior is habitual, you can speak up about it or choose to change agencies.

What will we talk about?

Be prepared with questions and to answer the agent's questions. Know what you want in your career and your agent. A word here: an agent is not your mother. She will not always be there to hold your hand. She will not always do the professional equivalent of packing your lunch, polishing your shoes and making sure your teeth are brushed. She may not even have the time to talk with you every time you want to talk- even sometimes when you feel you HAVE to talk. There are many other actors in the agency. Do not assume that once you have an agent you can sit back and shine. There is much work you need to do on your own.

Some agents may ask you to go home and write out your goals and objectives. This is another way the only marginally interested, lazy or out-of-touch can be separated from the truly dedicated, talented and hardworking actor. If the agent should require this, consider it a compliment and do it.

Agents' offices can be very busy, hectic places. A crisis happens every minute. Be prepared to wait your first time and just about every other time after that. Sometimes, true, it is mismanagement; but try to keep a cool head.

An agent may give you advice. There is a long-standing joke in Chicago that one veteran agent tells EVERYONE to cut their hair, pluck their eyebrows and lose ten pounds. If you like the agent and want to work with her take the advice. Often an agent will not like your pictures. That is a tough decision because pictures constitute a major outlay of funds. You often can negotiate with the agent to try to find a better shot from your proof sheet or work out an "easy time payment plan" with a photographer the agent recommends.

There have been cases in which an agent has been downright cruel to an actor. This does not happen often. What can happen is that an agent will call the situation as she sees it: that the actor is not talented, not marketable, not for her office. This can be told to the actor with greater or lesser degrees of tact and kindness. It is not what the actor wants to hear. Should this happen to you, try another agent. Remember, just like theatrical reviews, it is only one person's opinion. If, however, this is the opinion you meet consistently, a career redirection would be a very good idea. We are rarely our own best judges.

What if an agent wants money up front?

NEVER PAY TO PLAY. By that I mean you should NEVER have to pay money to sign with an agency. No reputable talent agency would dream of such a practice, but there are unscrupulous operations that spring up from time to time to prey off the eager and unsuspecting. Take comfort in the fact that eventually they all get closed down. You might consider checking out any of the lesser known agencies with the Better Business Bureau or the Illinois Department of Labor. The pay to play rule does NOT always apply to paying to be include in special marketing promotions some agencies put together: the agency directory or the agency voice-over reel.

What is exclusive versus multi-listing?

Here is a situation that does not arise in either New York or Los Angeles. In those cities actors may be represented by one agent for commercials, another for film and so on. Here in Chicago there is an option- if you are offered it.

Exclusive representation means exactly what it implies. You are represented for all work by one single agency. You MAY NOT take work through any other agency. Signing exclusively with one agency and then accepting work through another will earn the actor a heap of trouble and a shoddy reputation with other agents and casting directors. Think seriously before signing exclusive. Multi-listed means you may obtain work from any number of agencies with whom you are registered.

It is generally perceived that an agency will send its exclusives out first. Should they fit the role, they get first crack at it. That means often the only crack because casting directors will only see a certain number of actors for each role. Agents feel that since the exclusive actors have trusted them with their careers they, the agents, owe the actors this consideration.

This policy falls down however when an agency makes it a policy to sign armies of exclusives. Actors joke that signing with such an agency is tantamount to joining the Federal Witness Protection Program. The agent is perceived as being greedy, signing actors whether she plans to work for them or not, just to keep them from other agents. The actor gets lost in the hosts of other actors in his category. There is no time, with so many actors to deal with, to mold a career, to bring an actor along. These are isolated cases.

Some agencies, such as Jefferson and C.E.D. are exclusive only.

You need to know this before going to meet with them. And all agencies have their particular strengths. Some are strong on voice-over or industrial while others like to concentrate on film. Some offer representation in Los Angeles as well as Chicago. Some work with actor-writers, developing film and television projects. Some do a great deal of print, some none.

Perhaps the biggest question to answer before deciding the exclusive question is "What kind of work do I want to do?" All of the major agencies are asked to submit actors for most feature film and television work in Chicago. Some agencies have closer relationships with some casting directors but that is not a major concern.

Perhaps the biggest difference between agencies is in the voice-over and industrial departments. Not all jobs in these areas go to all agencies. Not all voice-over and industrial work is handled through casting directors. The voice-over and industrial departments of agencies establish relationships with various clients. Agents may work directly with advertising agencies, directors, producers or the company itself. TransGlobal Chemicals may only go to ABC Talent Agency for its industrial projects. Should you have no interest in doing voice-over or industrial work, this is, of course, not a concern. But for those who have aspirations in those areas it is a major consideration.

Once you have a longtime relationship with an agent and a foundation of mutual trust, you might negotiate an arrangement with your exclusive agent to free-lance your work in a certain area. That is to say, if the agency does not have a particularly active voice-over department you could switch your voice-over work to another agency or agencies while maintaining all your on-camera work with your long-term exclusive agent. This is not a standard arrangement.

How will I decide which agent is best for me?

Here are questions to ask yourself: How will this agency represent me? How many of my type are already signed? Does this agency get access to all the work I want in a particular field?

To answer the first question: does the agent see you exclusively as a 'character type' when you believe you can also play romantic leads? Is the agent willing to push you when the casting director doesn't initially request you? Your agent should be your champion. She should believe in you to the point that she will challenge the casting director's preconceptions of you. Additionally, she should fight to get you seen for roles that could be cast any number of ways.

Consider this scenario: a Made -For-TV movie is casting in Chicago and the cast breakdown includes a teacher, a store clerk, a judge and a motorist. If there is nothing in the script that says these characters must absolutely be white, thirty-year-old males, a good agent should try to convince the powers that be to see her clients who best match the personalities of the characters. There have been many cases where an agent who really knows and does her job has been able to turn what was written as a white male doctor into a Hispanic female doctor. Everyone benefits. This is an example of an agent really working as an agent, not an order taker.

Each actor is, of course, unique. You are you and no one else can be exactly what you are. Cast breakdowns are, however, far more general. They want types: McDonald's Counter Guy, Young Mom, CEO, Granny. Consider your age and your appearance. Of course you can play a number of types. The Mom In The Van for Burger King can also sometimes be the Upscale Corporate Woman for Ameritech. It's all a matter of perception: your agent's perception of you, the casting director's, the director's and the client's. It is only logical that if there are fewer of your "type" represented by an agency, you will get a bigger share of the auditions in your specific category as well as some cross-over auditions.

You might ask an agent tactfully why they are very heavy in a particular category. It may well be that the greatest percentage of the work may be in those categories. Logic also states that there are far more young actors in town so there will be more young actors registered. The ranks thin a bit as the ages increase. Actors either leave town or leave the business.

Does the agency have the work I want? As stated earlier not all voice-over and industrial work is available to all agencies. There are, however, many actors who work consistently in these areas while being represented exclusively by one agency. It is not an easy call. An actor must also consider that some agencies are more geared to film than others. Again you need to do research.

It is easy to be won over by an agent wanting to sign you exclusively. She is saying all the things you want to hear. But just as in any other major decision, consider all the options. Talk to other agents. Talk to clients of the agencies. Don't be discouraged if no one asks you to sign exclusively immediately. This is a very fluid market. Many things change. There is a rather high turnover rate among the staffs of talent agencies. Some agents leave the business or move to other agencies. Some go off on their own. Make it your business to know who is where.

Will there be a contract between me and the agent?

Should you accept exclusive representation you may be asked to sign a contract. In some cases a handshake suffices. Make sure the terms of any arrangements are well understood by both parties.

Take note of the length of the contract. Some agencies and actors decide to give it six months or so, with the understanding they will discuss mutual satisfaction with the arrangement at the end of that time.

What happens once I sign exclusively?

Once you are exclusive with an agency, you put that agency's name, address and phone number on your resume. It is your job to make sure that the agency name is on your resume. This is not the agent's job. If you have exclusive representation then by all means have the agency name printed on your resume.

You will leave twenty-five to fifty pictures and resumes with the agent. Check from time to time to see if she is running low. The office staff is often too busy to do this and you'd hate to miss out on a submission because they were out of your pictures. You and your agent also need to let the casting directors know that you are to be called by this agent only.

Be aware, too, that if you change your exclusive representation you must do several things. First you must tell the agent(s) you are leaving. This sounds fundamental, if not unpleasant. It can be an awkward, ugly scene. Some actors avoid it. They simply switch their allegiance to the new agency without informing the agent they are leaving behind. This is not only cowardice, it is bad business and earns the actor the reputation he or she deserves. Let the agent know in person, not by letter. Then collect your pictures. Let the casting directors know that you can be reached through the new agent. This is your responsibility.

How do I multi-list?

To register on a multi listed basis with other agencies, all you need do is fill out a registration form(s). You can have your resumes printed with no agency in the right hand corner and then place the agency sticker or stamp there yourself or you can have separate resumes printed with the names of each agency. Whatever you choose, it is your responsibility to have the agency's name on your resume.

It is wise to have a different color resume for each agency with that agency's name printed on it.. Keep careful record of who sends you out for each job. At auditions you are expected to sign in with your name, social security number, phone number, union affiliation and the agency that sent you. It is very important that you remember and record the correct agency. Confusion is no excuse.

What do I do after I'm registered?

Don't just sit back and wait for the telephone to ring. Get to know, as their schedules allow, everyone in the agent's office. This may not be easy because agencies are often overworked and under-staffed. Call in once a week to check in. Be prepared to hear "Nothing right now." But let them know you're out there.

An actor needs to do his or her own public relations work. Shameless self-promotion is not the agent's job.

Once you are in a play, don't just nag your agent(s) to see it, but also provide them with a rehearsal schedule, especially if you are rehearsing during the day as the majority of Equity shows do. Also let your agent know when you are going out of town or going to be away from your usual phone for any length of time. Leave her a number at which you can be reached should something wonderful turn up.

If an agency has booked you on a job which takes several days, remind them that you are unavailable for auditions or other work during that period. In an office where there are many agents, each handling a different department, your booking may not be common knowledge.

During the day, check your answering machine, your service or your beeper. These are all part of your job getting arsenal. Agents and casting directors get frustrated and angry when they have work for you and you are nowhere to be found. It gives the impression that you don't care.

Check with your agent before making any radical changes in your appearance. Remember that you need to look like your pictures. Men may need to grow facial hair for a play but be sure to let your agent know that you are now sporting a goatee. It can come as a shock to both casting director and agent if an actor shows up for an audition considerably furrier than either remembers. The local wisdom is that, except for character men, facial hair does not get you a lot of commercial or industrial work.

Never change your appearance between an audition and a call back, or between booking the job and doing it. Hell hath no fury like a director who hired a long-haired blonde and who, as the cameras are about to roll, is faced with a crew-cut brunette. The same goes for making changes during the run of a play.

Keep your resume updated and supply your agent with the updated copies. It is your job to make sure your agent(s) have a good supply of pictures.

If you have any questions about anything, check with your agent first. You may not get through immediately, but keep trying. If it is a true emergency let the office know. If not, don't cry wolf. They'll never answer your call again. It is always better to be doubly safe than to get into hot water. If you think you are going to be late for an audition call your agent and have her call the casting director. If you think you might have a product or schedule conflict, double and triple check it with the agent. If you have any questions about your union status, check with the agent. Better to be safe than sorry.

How does an agent get me work?

First, the agent gets you an audition. A typical scenario goes like this: The agent gets a call from a casting director giving the agent a "break down" (a list of the parts to be cast and a brief description of each character).

The casting director may add that the agent may only submit two actors for each role. This is not always the case but generally the numbers are limited. The casting director gives the time and place of the audition. If it is a commercial, the agent finds out any product conflict. You cannot do a spot for Pepsi if you have a spot currently on the air for Coke. Some conflicts are obvious, some surprising. The agent should find out what the conflicts are. If it is a commercial, a shoot date(s) will be given as well.

Usually the casting director will request specific actors. The agent can then make other suggestions, naming new actors or an established actor who the casting director didn't initially "see in the role." It is here that an agent can ask if the age, sex or race of the character is set in stone. The agent should know when and how far to push a casting director.

Next the agent calls the actor. When she does, listen carefully to what she says.

Agent: I have an audition for you.

Actor: Great. What?

Agent: It's for Ford. It's a national. (A commercial that is played nationally, as opposed to regionally or locally.)

Actor: I have no other car spots but I do have a John Deere thing running. Is that a conflict?

Agent: I doubt it but I'll check.

Actor: Thanks. Who am I?

Agent: You're a young dad on the weekend. Upscale but casual. You're shopping for a second car. A van.

Actor: When?

Agent. Monday eleven twenty.

Actor: Where?

Agent: Brolin's. You know they moved. You have the new number and address?

Actor: Yup. Thanks. Are there sides and where can I pick them up?

Agent: There's no copy yet. But she said it's only a couple of short lines. Get there ten minutes early, you should be fine.

Actor: When does it shoot and when are the call backs?

Agent: The call backs are Thursday and it shoots Wednesday or Friday of next week. That's the 6th or the 8th.

Actor: Here?

Agent: Yes, but out in Woodstock. Any problems?

Actor: Not a one. Thanks. Will the client be there? Is this going to be taped?

Agent: The client may be there but they will be taping anyway. Jane (the casting director) requested you specifically on this. Let me know how it goes.

Actor: Thanks. I sure will. Thanks again.

That's about how it goes, only generally both of you talk at the same time. Always find out where, when, what you're supposed to wear and whether or not there are "sides" or "copy" (the lines you will be asked to say). If there are sides, find out when and where you can pick them up. Check all product and time conflicts.

Find out if the audition is going to be taped. Certain colors look better on camera than others and women need to adjust their make-up. Black and white shoudl be avoided because they present such a high contrast to skin tones. So, no white shirts. This is particularly true for African-American actors. Additionally, high contrast small patterns (ie black and white checks or stripes) should be avoided because they play havoc with the camera.

Once again, if you have any questions about the job, ask them then and there. This is not, however, the time to discuss how well or poorly your career is going. The agent has other calls to make. If you're needing a chat with the agent, schedule it for another time.

Two things must be noted here. First, should your agent not be able to talk to you personally, she will leave a message on your answering machine or service. You must check in frequently and return calls promptly. An agent cannot confirm with the casting director that you will be at the audition at the scheduled time until she has talked with you. So call back immediately. Some casting directors have set cut off times for confirmations. That is to say that if by four o'clock Monday the agent cannot confirm that the actor will be at the call at 11:00 Tuesday, that audition slot is reassigned and that does not get to audition.

The other important protocol here is that if you are multi-listed, you must take the audition from the first agent who calls you. Once you are confirmed you cannot then switch agencies. Once again, be sure that when you sign in at an audition that you indicate the agency which sent you.

Actors must remember when scheduling auditions that each audition will last approximately sixty minutes. Don't expect to do an audition at 1:00 and then be on time for a 2:00 audition across town. You need travel time. Have your agent schedule your auditions so you can make all of them on time without worry.

Should a union audition run over one hour from your call time, you are entitle to compensation. It is good sense to report this to your agent.

Where do the auditions take place?

Sometimes auditions are held in the agent's office. A client may come in, usually for an industrial. Sometimes a casting director in Los Angeles will ask that the agent put auditions on tape and send them to her. Many agents, especially those with high powered voice-over departments, have their own sound studios and you will do a good percentage of your auditions at the office.

On other occasions the agent will be asked to submit a package of pictures and resumes to a casting director for a project, usually a film. These can go to one of the Chicago casting directors who will in turn show them to the director or the out-of-town casting director. From this meeting the decision is made as to which actors will be called in for an audition. Sometimes a local casting director is not used and the agent must submit to the out-of-town casting director.

Some out of town casting directors visit Chicago regularly. Los Angeles casting director Janet Hirschenson, who regularly casts for director John Hughes, is here at least a couple of times a year. She is a remarkable casting director with a keen eye and an impressive memory. She has established an excellent working relationship with many Chicago talent agents.

An agent will set up the auditions, juggling actors into the allotted time slots. If and whenever possible she or her assistant will notify the actor should there be a change in time or location. But changes are endemic to the business.

The subject of the audition will be covered in more detail later but accept the fact that if something can be changed it probably will be. It is part of the actor's job to be flexible. More often than not the change comes from the client. Everyone in the food chain, advertising agency types, directors, producers, casting directors, agents and actors are affected. The cooler everyone can stay the better. It is, after all, the client who is footing the bill and, as the saying goes, he who pays the piper... Unfair? Perhaps. But then, as your mother should have told you long ago, life is far from fair. Wonderful, but rarely fair.

What are callbacks?

Having called you for the audition, the agent will then call you should you get a callback. A callback is making the first cut. You will be asked to return and do the same thing or perhaps something different. All this will be discussed when we grapple with the audition chapter. Some agents like you to call to check in with them after you've finished an audition- especially if it is a very important one.

How will I know how I'm doing?

A good agent, when possible, will try to get feedback about the actor from the casting director or director. This is not always possible but it is invaluable when it does come through. The report is not always laudatory but the actor should nevertheless hear it and consider it. As with any opinion, the actor and her agent need to consider the source. What is behind the opinion? This information isn't always available. It may be a bad day. You may look just like the director's ex-lover. This you have no control over.

BUT some information is unbiased and concrete. If the casting director reports to the agent that you were late, rude, unprepared, uncooperative or couldn't take direction, that is something that need to be addressed immediately. Or she may say that the actor has talent but needs to do some more studying in on-camera technique. Sometimes a kind casting director will take the time from her frantic schedule to tell an agent that an actor is very good but has a funny little tick, a wandering eye or a habit of blinking too much. The actor needs to know this as well so that he or she can redress the situation.

On other occasions the casting director will be able to tell the agent that the client, director or producer really liked the actor but that they are "going a different way." They were looking for someone older, younger or from a different ethnic group. Often, too, you will hear praise. That makes your day.

Who decides how much I make for a job?

Should you book the job, the agent will then negotiate your contract. For on-camera work, an agent takes 10% as commission-THAT'S ALL. For print work an agent may take between 15-20%. A good agent will negotiate the best deal she can. That usually means getting you top dollar. When you have more work experience your agent can often ask a higher salary for you. The union sets the minimum salary for each job. This is referred to as "scale." Many jobs only pay scale, or scale plus ten (percent). This means that they, the client, are paying the agent's commission.

Sometimes a client will ask the agent what your "day rate" is for an industrial. This is a figure you and your agent need to decide on. She will then try to get it for you. You must trust your agent to negotiate the best deal possible for you. Remember that, as in trying to change the mind of a casting director, a good agent senses how far he or she can push.

Your agent will negotiate other things as well. If the job is for a film or television show, your agent may also discuss your billing, where your name comes in the credits. The more successful you become, the more you, through your agent, can negotiate.

What else can an agent do?

Some agents are willing to try to get auditions for plays (both union and non-union) for their clients. Ask your agent what her policy is in this matter. She will then negotiate your theatrical contract if you are cast in an Equity production.

You agent should help you map your career. She should let you know when you do well as well as when you mess up. Your agent should care about you enough to raise difficult issues when they need to be discussed. If you are getting in your own way by being unprofessional (late, unprepared, rude, uncooperative) they should call you on it. If you are getting too fat, need a haircut or a change of wardrobe, who better than your agent to point this out?

That is in the best of all possible worlds. Agents, even the best, don't always have the time. Their offices are busy, most times frantic. They have lives and crises too. Some who work as agents do not yet have the skills to do all that is required of an agent. But then not all actors, plumbers or doctors know or are capable of everything required of them. Do all in your power to sign with an agent who is an agent and not, as some in Chicago call them, "order takers."

What will an agent not do?

An agent will not be your mother, your therapist or your security blanket.

An agent cannot get you the job, only the audition. And even that not always. There are times when, no matter how hard the agent may try, a director will not see you.

An agent cannot always or habitually repair damage you have done by unprofessional behavior.

An agent cannot keep in her head flawless records of your schedule and product conflicts. You must be responsible for these. Nor can an agent be expected to remember your union status at all times. You need to be aware of where you stand.

An agent cannot be responsible for all your direct mailing pieces, though you should clear everything with her before sending it out.

An agent cannot make "them" give you a better costume.

Well, does the agent work for me or do I work for the agent?

You and your agent are a team. You are both human, subject to stresses and disappointments. You both have to know your business and act professionally. There is no perfect agent just as there is no perfect actor, doctor, lover or school. Your job is to find the one who best suits you and then work with mutual respect to make the partnership work. You work with each other, listening carefully to what the other says. Neither is boss. A good agent thinks of the actors she represents as her clients, not, as some agents say "my talent." You are not an agent's chattel nor is your agent your slave or whipping boy when you don't get the part.

Let your agent know how much you appreciate what she does for you. Not in a sycophantic way, but genuinely. Keep your part of the pact. And if you are unhappy about something, try to find out all the details. Possibly whatever went wrong was a miscommunication, a message not delivered or misunderstood. Clear the air before things begin to fester.

CASTING DIRECTORS

What is a casting director?

A casting director is the person who is responsible for bringing actors to the director, client or producer. This is done through the audition process.

She is NOT a casting AGENT. There is no such thing. For some reason people make this mistake. Now you don't have to.

And agents are not casting directors. In Chicago, you are one or the other.

What does a casting director do?

Casting directors in Chicago generally work with the directors and producers. This is the procedure for almost all commercials and industrials. This is also usually the case with any television series shot here. An outside (Los Angeles or New York) casting director may be brought in to help cast the "pilot," the initial episode of a series. But once the pilot is "picked up and goes to series," (bought by the network and scheduled to run on the air), the casting is handled locally.

When major films come to cast in Chicago, the director will often bring along a casting director. That out-of-town casting director may work in conjunction with a local casting director.

There are union and non-union casting directors in Chicago. There are casting directors who only cast extras for films, TV and commercials. There are casting directors who do not cast for film, only commercials and industrials.

An interesting note is that three of the major casting directors in Chicago are named Jane. It is a very good idea to keep them straight.

Do I contact casting directors directly, or wait for my agent to handle it?

In Chicago, casting directors keep extensive files of actors' pictures. When you get your pictures, send one copy to each casting director with whom you want to work. If you are a union member or have no interest in working as an extra, then there is no need to send to the non-union or extra casting directors. Always be sure your resume is attached. On the resume should be the name of the agent through whom you want to be called.

Extra casting directors will NOT call through a talent agency so you need to give them your own telephone number. Just write it on your resume if it is not printed there anyway.

What if my pictures or resumes change?

When you update your resume or your pictures, send one copy of the update to the casting directors. Why one copy? Unlike the agents, that's all they need. And their files can only hold so many. When you go in for an audition you will bring another copy to be used for that particular job. The casting director will always request a picture from the agent before the audition. Save the pictures, paper and stamps.

What exactly happens before the casting director auditions actors?

The casting director will receive a breakdown of roles to be filled from the director or producer. They will agree on a time and location for the audition. Sometimes the director, producer or client are at the initial audition. Sometimes they only appear at the callbacks. Naturally, if the director is unavailable for the first audition your work will be video-taped. Often your work, even with the director present, will be taped. Callback and casting decisions are made by watching the tapes and referring to your headshots. That is why you should always bring extra copies of your headshot to the callback.

If the director is from Chicago or has worked in Chicago frequently (as have Andrew Davis and John Hughes), they may request that certain actors be called in. The casting director reads the breakdown and makes a list of actors she believes would be good for the roles. Your agent may also make suggestions. A good agent will know how to push a casting director to see an actor not already on the list. She will also know when to stop pushing.

What if I hear about something I haven't been called to audition for?

If you are interested in a project (film, TV show) you need to call your agent to find out if there is anything for you. Agents generally hate this, unless of course you have a specific role in mind and that role is not the lead.

Agents hate being pestered by every actor on their books BUT since you cannot call the casting directors...

You never call casting directors. Not ever. You can write to invite them to a play you are in but the rule in Chicago is that you never call.

Casting directors are very powerful in Chicago. They can get you into or keep you out of an audition. They are human and have their good and bad days. Some show it more than others. You need them, so be polite. If you have a gripe, take it up with your agent. Some actors have personality conflicts with certain casting directors and choose not to go on calls from that office. If the casting director isn't particularly fond of you, you may not get the chance to turn down an audition.

Be polite, pleasant, professional. Don't grovel or be sycophantic. That's just as hateful.

What if the casting director is behaving unprofessionally?
This is a sticky point.

There have in the past been complaints of unprofessional behavior by casting directors. In one instance, a self-styled casting director auditioned actresses for a low budget horror film. Actresses later complained that he asked them, pressured them, to remove layers of clothing. He also made sexual advances. This kind of behavior is rare but it does occur and it is completely reprehensible.

Anyone who is made to feel uncomfortable should know that they can walk out immediately. The behavior should then be reported to the agent and to the union if this was a union call. Having a union to whom you have recourse is great. The work doesn't get away with the behavior. Report any abuse. Do not be a victim. No job is worth it.

Do I thank the casting director for booking me? And how?

You can, after you've been booked through a casting director's office, send a note of thanks. Some actors will also send flowers or a token of thanks. A note is really all that's needed.

Are there things casting directors hate?

ACTORS WHO:

- have a bad attitude
- arrive late- or way too early
- hang around the waiting room and talking loudly
- do not listen to the directions
- do not know their union status, time or product conflicts
- do not have the money or desire to join the union when they are at a 'Must Join' status
- do not remember which agent sent them
- are rude to staff and interns
- do not know what audition they were sent on
- do not fill in all the sign-in forms
- lie- anywhere, anytime, about anything
- call and ask "Why wasn't I seen for this?"

UNIONS

What are the unions I need to know about?

That very much depends on what you want to do.

What about stage work, being in plays?

The Actors' Equity Association is the union for stage actors. Unlike New York City where just about all the stage work is union, there is a great deal of non-Equity, non-union, work in Chicago.

Union and non-union theatre get approximately the same press coverage, though the Equity theatres are generally the larger companies. In Chicago there is a new storefront theatre company opening (and, alas, also closing) just about every week. Young actors come to Chicago from all over the map because of the opportunities afforded here.

An actor can work in these non-union houses until he joins the union. Once you join Actors' Equity you cannot accept any non-union acting or stage managing work.

A member of Equity can, however, <u>direct</u> in a non-union theatre.

Can a non-union actor get a job as an actor at a union theatre?

A non-Equity actor can work in an Equity theatre. Quite often smaller roles are offered to non-union actors. The availability of non-union roles depends on the contract under which the theatre is operating. All Equity theatres must abide by Equity rules. Most not-for-profit Equity theatres in Chicago are allowed to hire non-union actors. The number of non-union actors allowed depends on the size of the cast and the scale of contract under which they operate with Actors' Equity. Confusing? Yes.

Here's an example. The size of the theatre, number of seats and number of performances a week determine the contract for a union theatre. So, let's say a not-for-profit union theatre with under 200 seats, scheduling eight performances a week, is planning to do *King Lear*. Unless this is some radical concept production using puppets and masks and film (don't laugh, it's been tried) they will need some twenty actors. The number of Equity contracts offered (union actors hired) may vary but there will be approximately eight or more non-union contracts that can be offered under this scenario. It's a good bet that the role of King Lear is not going to be one of them, or Glouschester. But there are all those Attendant Lords and France and Burgundy. Perhaps even Cordelia could be cast non-Equity.

Who usually gets the non-union roles?

The acting pool in Chicago is rich in young actors, and the younger roles are often cast with non-union actors. As actors mature, and stay in the business, they almost inevitably join Equity, thus the pool of non-union actors over forty is considerably smaller. Actors either join Equity, move out of town or they give up the business for a more reliable career.

Those who give up acting to support themselves and their families sometimes return later in life. Chicago actors with national recognition such as Mike Nussbaum and Nate Davis did just that.

Some actors decide not to join the union at all. They want to be acting as often as possible. Non-union theatres afford them more frequent opportunity. They must, however, have some other means of supporting themselves. Union theatre pay is pitiful, non-union theatre pay is virtually non-existent.

When are rehearsals if I have to have another job?

Because non-Equity theatre actors must have some other means of support, rehearsals are at night and on the weekends. Rehearsal periods for non-union theatre are often longer. Union theatres rehearse during the day and generally only rehearse for two to three weeks before going into preview performances.

Read carefully the above statement about staying non-union.

To stay non-union for any great period of time you must concentrate your work in non-union houses.

How do I become a member of Actors' Equity?

When a non-union actor works in an Equity house, he begins to accumulate Equity Membership hours. You must register as an Equity Membership Candidate and keep track of your weeks worked in Equity theatres. When you have accumulated a certain number of weeks, you will join the union with your next Equity contract. You must be aware of your standing so as not to embarrass yourself or a potential employer.

You can also qualify as an Eligible Performer, which would allow you to audition for Equity productions along with Equity actors but not actually be a member of the union yourself. The rules for becoming Eligible revolve around having been paid the minimum eligible rate for four consecutive weeks as a performer at a professional theatre (not amateur or community) or in motion pictures, television or radio. The equivelant minimum pay scale depends on the calendar year in which the work was done. If you think you may qualify contact the local Equity office. You must be able to verify the employment before Equity will bestow Eligible status.

As mentioned earlier, some actors choose to stay out of the union indefinitely. They feel that joining the union will limit the work they can do because there is more non-union work in Chicago than there is union work. This is a sensible decision if all they want to do is act for the sake of acting. But they do in essence limit themselves. They must be careful not to accrue too many Equity hours. This will limit the roles they can take in Equity theatres.

The general wisdom in Chicago is that young actors, or ones just moving to Chicago, would do well to stay non-union for the first couple of years. They can spend this time making a name for themselves in the many non-union companies and in playing the smaller or younger roles in the union houses. This way they get the recognition they need for the professional theatres to notice and hire them and they are accruing Equity hours.

Should I even bother taking small roles with the small theatre companies?

Theatre in Chicago relies heavily on networking. It is a scary business and directors and producers are risking a great deal every time they put up a production. They are more likely to go with a known actor, one with whom they have worked or with whom friends of theirs have worked, than an unknown quantity. Therefore, the more work you do in good companies may well lead to more work. Groups form and disband but members of companies will remember each other and call upon those who have proved themselves not only talented but professional.

As mentioned earlier, there is a pyramid of actors in Chicago. The greatest number of non-union actors is in the twenty to thirty-five age range. Union theatres will often use their non-Equity contracts for these younger roles. Directors and producers in Chicago go to see Chicago theatre. The artistic staff of Equity theatres make it a point to see non-union productions. Besides, good credits on your resume give directors a sense of your work and provide references for you.

So, should I join Equity or not?

Some theatres use no non-Equity actors at all. In the houses which do hire non-union actors, some casts are so small that all the roles must be Equity. Not joining the union is no guarantee that you will work consistently, but then, neither is joining the union. So many factors go into casting.

Once an actor joins Equity, it must be repeated, he can no longer work outside union jurisdiction. There are many advantages to joining the union when the time comes. Among those benefits are: Equity wages are higher, the hours are strictly regulated, your pay and safe working conditions are insured. You can also qualify for pension and welfare benefits and insurance.

What do union actors do when they aren't in a show?

Equity does allow a great deal of freedom for Equity actors to do showcases and readings. A showcase is a production featuring Equity actors which runs for a limited period and for which the actors receive no pay. More and more union actors are exercising this option to produce works which would not otherwise be performed.

Staged readings are also becoming popular. Equity allows its actors a limited number of performances and there is a small stipend paid. Equity Library Theatre produces as well. These productions are often classics such as Shakespeare.

Where do I find more specific information on membership?

An actor interested in joining Actors' Equity should call the Chicago office for a copy of the most up-to-date requirements and dues schedule. There is a sizable initiation fee. Sometimes arrangements can be made with the theatre that casts you in your first Equity role for your union initiation fee to be paid directly to Equity out of your paychecks. You may want to make other arrangements.

Once you are a member, you will receive a bill for dues twice a year. Union dues must be paid on time, otherwise there can be serious and damaging consequences. You must bring your up-to-date Equity card to all auditions and show it to the monitor.

Whether or not you choose to join Equity, whenever you join, it is wise to know all about the union from the very beginning of your career in Chicago. Only when you know what you options are can your make informed choices.

Know what your union status is at all times. Indicate it on your resume. If you have any questions, call the union.

What about unions for film and television actors?

The two other unions with which Chicago actors need to be very familiar are the Screen Actors Guild (SAG) and American Federation of TV and Radio Artists (AFTRA). These are the unions for television commercials and programs, radio spots (voice-overs), industrials and films.

Like Actors' Equity these unions were established to protect the actors' rights and safety. The unions set the number of hours allowed on a day's worth of shooting and the minimum rates an actor is to be paid for his work.

Unions negotiate pay for work done overtime. They set the standards for safety. It is to them that an actor can complain if he is not receiving his residuals or his session fee is late. They keep track of earnings and oversee the pension, welfare and insurance.

Can I do any film or television without being in these unions?

There is non-union commercial and industrial work in Chicago. And there are non-union agents and casting directors to deal with it. For the most part, non-union work is safe, especially the older, established firms. You will not be exploited and you will be paid. If you get ripped off working outside of the union you can go to the State of Illinois Board of Labor with your grievance.

While there are many legitimate operations, non-union film, commercial and industrial work is notorious for scams and snakes. The actor and the agent need to be very, VERY careful.

Here's another non-union commercial warning. Beware of doing non-union work in mahor categories - eg fast food. If you are a classic McDonald's counterperson or young parent type and have done a non-union fast food spot this eliminates you from consideration for any other fast food spot while the non-union spot is running. One classic perfefct McDonald's mom did a non-union Subway spot which ran for five years. She was paid $500 for the buyout and by doing so, according to one of Chicago's top casting directors, lost at $10,000 in bookings she would have got. "She was tht good."

When do I have to join SAG or AFTRA?

You do NOT need to join the union on your first union job. You can work under what is called a Taft Hartley Agreement. If you are booked as a principal in a union commercial, you can shoot it without joining the union if you work under a Taft Hartley. BUT you must join the union 30 days after the first union job, if you want any more union jobs. For 30 days from the day you sign the Taft Hartley you may do as many union or non-union jobs as you like without having to join SAG or AFTRA. Any union job booked on the 31st day or later neccessitates you joining the union. If union information is asked for on a casting director's sign-in sheet you MUST indicate that you are working under a Taft Hartley and are, therefore, a MUST JOIN or must pay. That means that you must join on your next booking.

It is a very good rule to follow that you put aside your earnings from your first union job as a down payment (or full payment) on your initiation and dues when you must join. Very little makes casting directors more irate than actors who are Must Joins and who, when presented with the opportunity to join, cry that they do not have the money. Don't spend that money. Put it aside and have it ready.

A general rule to follow in determining under which union's jurisdiction a job will fall is hat SAG covers work on film and AFTRA covers work on videotape.

SAG also covers some extras in commercials. When many, many extras are used some may be non-union. The pay per day is predetermined, along with overtime, meal penalties and all other charges. Extras, however, do not get residuals. SAG members have only recently been able to work as extras and it's a handy way to pick up a quick couple of hundred dollars. Union commercial extra work should not be confused with film extra work, which is usually not union related and pays considerably less.

As with Actors' Equity, once you have joined, keep your dues paid up. You must be a member in good standing to work. Some casting directors will ask you on their sign-in sheets if you are a fully paid up union member or not. Just like Equity, once you are a union member you may NOT do any non-union work. That's scabbing and is a serious violation. It's not worth it to try to get away with it. You will be caught eventually.

What about student or educational films?

SAG does make some concessions (SAG waivers) on film work, especially on student films. Union actors can work for little or no money on these student or independent projects but all the paper work must be cleared through the union.

As with Equity, if you have any questions at all, call the union. If you think something may not be on the up and up or are asked to work non-union and the producers tell you it's been cleared with the union, check it out.

TOOLS OF THE TRADE

What does an actor in Chicago need?

Just as in any other profession, there are tools of the trade. A good workman keeps these with him and always in good repair. Without them, you will miss out on or lose work. With them, you can make your dream happen.

Here is a list. Each will be explained separately.

1. A good quality, up-to-date attractively printed resume.
2. Good quality, up-to-date professional pictures. Note that this is plural.
3. An excellent, high-quality professional voice tape (if you plan to do voice-over).
4. A reliable answering machine, service, beeper or mobile phone.
5. Good maps of Chicago and suburbs.
6. A versatile wardrobe.
7. An ear prompter. (if you plan to do industrials).

What is a good resume and how do I get one?

Each agent has her own particular opinions about resume styles. These are variations on a standard theme. Be prepared to adjust your resume to meet your agent's requirements. This is easy if you have it prepared on a computer.

Whatever the variations, there are two basic rules for a resume. One, it has to be true. Two, it has to be printed legibly and cut to 8'x10" and affixed to your picture. There is no getting around those two rules.

It has to be true because if you lie you will be found out. Who, then, will want to hire a liar? There are two forms of lying: saying you did something you didn't and saying you can do something you can't.

Do not pad your resume. If it looks short because you are just starting out, don't worry. Everyone was once just starting out. There will always be actors out there with more experience than you and there will always be ones with less. Don't be tempted to a) invent theatre companies and say you worked with them, b) say you were in productions you were not, c) say you played a role other than the one you did, or d) represent scenes done in class or workshops as full productions.

This is a very small community, the acting world. Someone will inevitably know that you are lying because they saw, were in or directed the production about which you are fibbing. And don't, for instance, say you can speak fluent French if you cannot. Before too very long, someone will call you on it and there you will be 'avec les oeufs sur votre visage.'

Do not say that you are a singer or a dancer unless you are regularly performing or taking classes in those areas.

There is a standard format for resumes in Chicago. Everyone expects the resume to be computer-generated. It's easy to set-up, easy to read and easy to update. There are many resume services for actors. Act I Bookstore's Resume Service has become the unofficial headquarters over the past several years.

Laser printing gives resumes a good, crisp look. Printing on recycled paper, like that available at the many Kinkos stores, is a very nice touch. Stick with white, off-white, cream, light grey or blue. Neon paper may make an impact, but not the one you hoped for. Remember: resumes are your business cards. They need to look professional.

Always have resumes cut to 8'x10" - the size of the standard headshot. You can either glue or staple the resume to the back of the headshot, but it must be attached securely. Some printers, such as National Photo Service will actually print the resume on the back of the photo. But be aware that you will be updating your resume, hopefully, more often than you run new pictures.

The set-up of a resume is simple.

Your name goes at the top in large letters. Use whatever name you are planning to use professionally. Think hard about this. Before you start establishing a name for yourself, find out if someone else has been using it before you. The unions will only allow one person to use a name. It would be confusing and inconvenient to have to change your name a couple of years from now.

If your name really is Elizabeth Taylor or Michael Jackson, you know already you're going to have to add a middle name or change some part of it. Actors and singers are obvious. But you might give some thought to a name alteration if you sport the same moniker as an athlete. They too have to join the unions when they make commercials (and all that money).

A quick call to the unions will tell you if your name is already on their books. They will be able to tell you just how different your name will have to be to avoid confusion.

The New York actor W.H. Macy was once the Chicago actor Bill Macy in the long-ago days when we were both doing David Mamet premieres in what became the celebrated Chicago off-loop theatre movement. Bill became W.H. because there was a television actor called Bill Macy who played Bea Arthur's husband on "Maude." Now W.H. is the big star and does Mamet premieres on Broadway.

Think twice about using nicknames. It may be cute and catchy now, but you're hoping this career will last a lifetime. When they hand out the Oscar, the Tony or the lifetime achievement award, Margaret or Robert will look a great deal more immortal than Muffy and Biff.

Time was when actors born with names that were difficult to spell or pronounce, or names that they thought were clumsy or just plain, changed them. That's not the case now, at least in Chicago. Credits read like a United Nations.

Whatever you come to call yourself, your name goes, in large letters, in the center, at the top of the resume. Underneath it you list your unions. If you are an Equity Membership Candidate (EMC) you may choose to indicate that. If you have no union affiliations, leave the space blank. Don't panic. You'll get them.

Whatever you do, don't put "Actor" or "Actress/Singer/Dancer." It says amateur. We know what you do. We didn't send out a call for auto mechanics.

To the left put your height, weight, hair and eye color and social security number. Do not put your sizes on your resume. When you go to an on-camera audition there may be a size card to fill out (see Audition chapter). If you are a model as well as an actor, the size information will be on your composite. Size information does not belong on a resume.

What about listing my age or age range?

DO NOT LIST YOUR BIRTH DATE. No one needs to know how old you are. You can be whatever age they need you to be. Let them decide from your audition if you are the right age for the role, don't prejudice them. If they do ask, don't lie. The exception here is child actors, who should put their birth date up in the corner by their height and weight.

Once again, when you go to an on-camera audition in Chicago there will be a sign-in sheet on which, along with other information, you will be asked to mark your gender, race and whether you are under or over 40. This information is for the unions. Otherwise, there is no need to limit yourself by putting that information on the resume.

Don't put in your "age range" either. Let them decide. Directors might misconstrue that you are either telling them how to look at you or doing their job for them.

If you are a strong singer, indicate your range.

The right hand side of the resume is for agent information. In

Chicago, if you are represented exclusively by one agent, then have that agent's name, address and phone and fax numbers printed on the right hand side; using the agent's logo or typeface is a nice touch. If you are multi-listed, leave the space blank and then take the resumes to each agent's office where you will put in the appropriate agent's name and address using a stamp or labels.

NEVER PRINT YOUR HOME ADDRESS AND TELEPHONE NUMBER ON YOUR RESUME. You have no idea into whose hands these resumes may wander. This is especially true for women. All non-theatre work should be handled by the agent. You can, and should, write your telephone number on your resume for theatre auditions. In Chicago this is the accepted policy. Everyone expects a hand-written phone number on a printed resume. It doesn't look slip-shod, it looks smart.

Is it better to put on-camera work or stage experience first?

If you are interested in both theatre and commercial (film, TV, commercials, etc.) work, you may choose to have two resumes. This is not necessary but, in Chicago, it is an option. The difference in the two resumes would be the order in which you place your theatrical and on-camera experience. If you are preparing a theatrical resume, you list your theatre experience first. If you want a resume to represent you for film and television, then list those two categories first and follow them with theatre.

Whichever category you choose to lead off your resume, the criteria for the listing of the experience is the same. As you can see on the example, each heading is given in bold, large letters. Then you need to list the experience. Again, be honest. No matter how good it would look on the resume, if you didn't really do it, don't put it on.

In Chicago, agents suggest that you lead off your lists with your strongest work, even if it is not necessarily your most recent. Ideally your most recent roles are your strongest but that's not always the case. Directors will not always have time to read all the way down a resume, so grab their attention in the first couple of lines. If you choose to list Feature Film first, then set up this section by listing the project, the role, the studio and the director, in that order. Again, put your strongest work first. If you don't have Hollywood-class credits, but you do have independent or student film work to show, by all means list that.

It is important to list the director because very often the person with whom you are interviewing for work will know the director or have seen her work. It can give you and the interviewer something to talk about. Additionally, if needed, the prospective employer can call the director and ask about your work.

If you are preparing an on-camera resume, follow Feature Film credits with Television. Follow the same format as you did with Feature Film.

The next category is theatre. Again, the standard form is play, role, theatre. The director's name, if you'd like, can come before or after the theatre column. Your strongest work goes first. For aesthetics, you may want to list all productions with one theatre company together.

Should I include work I've done as an extra?

Some professionals say to include it, some not. Ask your agent. If you have other work, list that work first. Then, if you need the additional credits or if all you have is extra work, list that. Do not be ashamed if all you have is extra work. Everyone has to start somewhere. As you get more work you will add the new roles and gradually ease the extra work off the resume. In the meantime, listing extra work says to a director that you are eager to work and to learn. It says that you have been on and around a film set and know the ropes, the protocols, the rules- like the golden rule that the crew eats first. Do not list more than 5 or so extra jobs though or you begin to look like a professional extra.

Do I list roles if I was an understudy?

If you understudied a role but never went on, you may include that role but you must indicate your understudy status by putting (US) next to the role. If you did go on, you may list the role without any notations.

Awards or premieres?

A world, American or even regional premiere can be indicated in parentheses under the name of the production. If you won an award for the role, you can indicate that either by putting an asterisk next to the listing and noting the award further down the resume or by mentioning the award in parentheses under either the role or the production.

Should I list college and high school credits?

If that is all you have, by all means include it. As I've said earlier, everyone has to start somewhere. The same can be said of ensemble or chorus work in a production. Include it. Soon the principal roles will come along and you can delete the other work.

Those with a strong musical theatre history may want to make separate categories for musicals and straight plays. The same holds true for revue or comedy (stand up or improvisational) work.

Do I list commercials and industrials by client?

Some agents and casting directors say yes, some no. The argument for listing is to show your experience. The argument against is that should you be up for a McDonald's spot the client may choose someone else if he sees work for Burger King on your resume.Listing production houses, ad agencies and/or directors is a safer choice.

My advice is that you ask your agent and follow her advice. Many people with extensive commercial and industrial credit simply put a line on their resumes saying "Commercial/Industrial list available on request." But don't say this if you don't have one when it's required. If you have a voice tape or an on-camera reel you can indicate that in a similar manner.

Why should I list my education and training?

Many casting directors in Chicago, as well as across the country, like to see where you received your training. The next category on your resume, after the camera and stage credits, should be training. List the sort of training and the teacher. You may choose to include the school as well. It is generally agreed that you should not list the length of time you studied or the exact year. Here again, your agent will guide you.

Special Skills?

The last category on the Chicago actor's resume is the area in which you can list any extraordinary talent you have: a language you speak fluently, the ability to drive an eighteen wheeler, deliver a calf or eat fire. Think about the things, ordinary or uncommon, you can do that someone might need you to do on stage or in a film.

The rule here is not to include something unless you really can do it, do it well and do it at the drop of a hat. That is to say, don't include juggling or unicycle riding if you can only just sort of do it.

List your dialects if you do any- WELL. List languages you speak- FLUENTLY. List sports you play well- the more unusual first. Include musical instruments you play well and dance forms in which you are proficient.

Things not to include are driving a car (just about everyone can except me) or hobbies like reading, knitting, traveling or cooking. You don't want to list typing but you might include court reporting.

Do not include references. Your credits and training will speak for you.

What is a good headshot and how do I get one?

This is not nearly as easy a question to answer. But like a resume, a headshot is an indispensable tool. You are often given or denied an audition on the strength of your picture. Film work, especially, is all about "look."

A good headshot is one that looks like the you who is going to walk into the audition. By that I mean not some over glamorized you or one in which your hair is both a different length and style than the one you now sport. Nor one ten pounds lighter or heavier than your current weight.

A good commercial headshot is not necessarily a good theatrical or film headshot. In Chicago, most actors have at least one of each. A professional photo session will yield two or three pictures and runs somewhere in the neighborhood of $200. That generally includes shooting two to three rolls of film and the photographer giving you anywhere from two to four prints. That does NOT include make-up, retouching or printing copies.

What's a commercial headshot like?

In a good commercial headshot you should look, not surprisingly, like people in commercials. Spend time watching commercials to catch the look. As a rule, commercial headshots are "brighter," more cheerful, smilier than theatrical shots. They are casual in feeling, as though you were just out buying that car, house, cereal or beer.

Those looking to do "glamour" spots should have a high fashion look as well. This is not to be confused with the All American commercial shot.

Would an industrial headshot be different?

Industrial headshots go for a corporate look- the suit, the glasses. If you don't intend to do industrials, you will not need one of these. But remember, Chicago is a big market for industrials. You won't always be called upon to play "some guy in a suit talking about dental plans or the new K37Vh20 system" but you may be submitted for a doctor, lawyer, teacher, scientist and it helps to have a "business look" as one of your headshot options.

And for film or theatre?

Your theatre or film headshot can be more dramatic, less commercial. In Chicago the three-quarter (3/4) shot is very popular. This is a picture that features you from approximately the knees up. The 3/4 shot is used for both commercial and film pictures; but most agents will tell you that if you choose to use the 3/4 format for one of your shots, the other should be a standard headshot.

Your agent will tell you what she wants for each look and well as her favorite photographers. In Chicago, the formula is to call and schedule visits with several photographers. At these meetings you get to look at a portfolio of actors headshots. You should also discuss what you want from your pictures. It is important that you like both the photographer and her work. You'll be investing a great deal of money in these pictures so choose someone who does good work and with whom you have a rapport.

If I'm just starting out do I really need such expensive pictures?

DON'T GET CHEAP PICTURES. Cheap pictures look exactly like what they are. It is a classic example of false economy to go for cheap pictures. They scream amateur. No matter how nice the pictures Uncle Louie took at Cousin Maude's wedding, they are not professional headshots. There is a particular look to professional headshots. You need to get them from someone who knows what she's doing.

And don't confuse portraits with headshots. There are many excellent, experienced and expensive photographers out there but they do not all shoot headshots for the Chicago acting market. They do not know what agents and casting directors want. Spend your money wisely. Ask the agents for recommendations. Check out the photographers. Make your selection and set a date.

How do I prepare for the photo session?

Don't stay out swilling beer all night before the shoot. If you know there are times you look better than others, schedule accordingly. If you're a morning person, try to arrange a morning shoot. Do whatever you can to look your best.

Which brings us to make-up. Most photographers have a make-up person with whom they work. If you are going to wear make-up for the shoot, and most women do and should, it is wise to book a make-up person. Headshots are always black and white photography so remember the make-up is different from stage and street make-up. Spend the extra money to have it professionally applied. It is well worth it. The make-up person will also look after your hair.

What should I wear to the shoot?

You'll carry several outfits to the shoot and you and the photographer will choose what will look best. Your favorite ensemble may not photograph well, not matter how much you like it. Take the photographer's advice. If you have a relationship with an agent already, ask her advice.

It will take a little while after the shoot for the photographer to develop the proof sheets. These are very small prints of each shot. The photographer may mark the ones she likes best. You then take the proof sheets and a loupe (asmall magnifying glass) to your agent(s) to get their choices. This isn't always easy. Agents within an office may not agree. Agents from different agencies may not agree. You may hate all of the choices. That's a dilemma. But remember, it will be the agents and not you who send out the picture. If they don't like the pictures, they may be reluctant to push them. You may wind up with a headshot you think is swell that sits in the agent's drawer.

Now, if your agent hates the pictures and you went to a photographer that she recommended, your agent can ask the photographer to reshoot you at no additional cost. This happens. Not all that often, but it happens. The photographer relies on the agent to send him clients and will want to keep in her good graces. This doesn't work if it is just you who hates the pictures.

What about retouching or fixing the photo after it is taken?

A retoucher can airbrush out strange shadows, a dark circle under the eye or the pimple that arrived just in time for the shoot.

You may be tempted to erase all the wrinkles, all the lines. Don't. Your pictures have to look like you or they are no good. Ask your agent's advice about retouching and then go to one recommended by the agent or photographer. Once again, don't cut corners. Go to the best.

Where do I get the pictures run off?

Once you and your agent have decided on the shots you will use and you've visited the retoucher, take the prints to a top notch photo service to have them reproduced. Again, this is not a place to look for a cheap price. This is an expensive process but necessary. They will make a negative of your prints and then reproduce from that negative. You will want at least a hundred of each picture.

You can choose to have your pictures printed with either a matte or a glossy finish. You can have your name printed on the picture. The pictures can have a border or be borderless. Here again, take the agent's advice. Some agents ask that you not put your name on your pictures. They feel that this forces the director to turn the picture over and read your resume. Other agents disagree. Some casting directors suggest you have some printed with your name and make sure that one goes to the casting directors. Then every time they go through their files your face <u>and</u> name will be put in front of them. That's how they learn who are the new actors.

Some reproduction houses will print your resume on the back of your picture. Some people seem to like this but others argue that it makes it difficult and expensive to update your resume.

You can have postcards made with your photograph on them. These are handy for sending out to casting types when you are in a play or film and want to let them know about it.

How often will I need new pictures?

In Chicago the average life of headshots is about two years. That is to say, approximately every eighteen months you need to get new ones taken. Some casting directors will argue that you need to replace them more frequently. No doubt others will say that if the pictures still look like you, you can get another year or so out of them. You absolutely need new pictures if you change your size, appearance or are looking to break into a new market- or want to be reconsidered in the old ones.

What do I do with the pictures after I have copies?

Once your headshots are attached to your resumes, deliver about twenty-five of each look to your agent(s). And make sure that they don't run out of them. You may also send out pictures to casting directors and artistic directors. The others you keep on hand to take to auditions <u>and call backs</u>.

It is a very good idea to ALWAYS have pictures and resumes with you. You never know who you are going to run into or when your agent is going to need to run to an audition. If you have to schlep all the way back home for the picture, you may just miss the job.

What is a voice tape and do I need one?

The voice tape is the equivalent of a headshot for the voice-over performer; a short cassette tape recording of you performing the voice-over scripts for a number of sample commercials. If you are interested in working in this field you MUST have a great voice tape. An adequate voice tape won't do. This is a fiercely competitive market and quality really pays off.

This, too, is a very expensive undertaking. You have to pay good money to get a good tape. There are low-budget operations but, once again, you get what you pay for.

Work only with a good, reputable producer. Ask your agent for suggestions. Her opinion will be highly subjective so you need to meet with the producer before beginning to work. As with a photographer, the two of you must have a special rapport. The producer must produce a tape tailored for you, your strengths, your personality. Beware of tapes that sound like everyone else. A really good producer will write the copy JUST FOR YOU- not pull it out of a file used for everyone.

Since this is a very expensive project, it is wise to determine if it is worth the expense. A good producer will meet to talk with you and give you an honest opinion of your chances.

What exactly is on a voice tape?

It's best to start by saying that a tape should be approximately two and a half minutes long. No more. The selections should be short, should show the variety of your voice and should sound like actual commercials. Some people choose to have a couple of spots with dialogue on their tape. The producer should arrange the tape so that it flows smoothly and highlights your versatility.

Once you make the tape (for which you will pay for the producer, engineer and studio time), you will need to have it reproduced. This too can run into serious money. Once again, go for quality. Ask the producer for suggestions. Your name needs to be on the tape itself. You can either have it printed on the tape or on a gummed label that is then affixed to the tape. Your name and your contact number must be on the tape itself, because the tape may stray from its box.

As for the box, you will need a J card. What, you may well ask, is a J card? It is that piece of paper somewhat shaped like a J that sits in the plastic box and forms the label. It should have a catchy graphic on the cover. Your name and your agent's name and numbers should be on the side.

You can even put more information on the back or inside. This information can include your name and agent's name, contact numbers, the producer, the engineer and maybe a list of the commercials you are doing. It's just like the J cards used in music cassettes. The key words here are "quality catchy graphic."

You will need to go to a graphic artist to work out your logo. Many people use a pun on their name or a catchy phrase or slogan.

The idea here is to attract attention to the tape so that it will be played by the people who are in a position to hire you.

Why does the tape need to be so catchy, slick and professional looking?

Because these people are deluged with tapes and listening to new tapes is something they relish about as much as gum surgery.

Once your tapes are ready they need to be delivered to your agent's office. If you have more than one voice-over agent, make sure that the appropraite agent's name is on the tapes you leave at that office. And make sure that when you go out on an audition you not only remember which agent sent you out, you also carry with you copies of the tape with that agent's name on them.

As with pictures, never leave the house without copies of your tape.

Are there other places I can distribute the tapes?

Chicago is a mecca for advertising agencies and a great many tapes will go to the creative staffs there. Others will go to producers. More about this in the voice-over chapter.

Remember- your voice tape often IS your audition. Make it the best one you can.

Why do I need an answering machine, service, beeper or mobile phone?

This is a very simple question to answer- because agents need to get in touch with you RIGHT AWAY. It does absolutely no good to have great pictures and resumes, a whizbang voice tape and be in universal demand if no one can find you. Things in Chicago happen in a split second and if you don't get the message you don't get the job.

A good answering machine is the bottom line. This presumes you have a phone and that you've paid the bill. Go hungry but pay the phone bill. Call waiting and voice mail are both helpful innovations and worth checking into.

Don't rely on anyone else to take your messages. Don't have calls sent to your great aunt's house or the pub down the road. Likewise, if your house mates (be they family, roommates or significant others) cannot be relied upon to take messages well, instruct them to leave the answering machine on.

You may have to get your own line with your own answering machine if your roommates have a habit of erasing your messages while retrieving theirs. It's worth it.

Get an answering machine from which you can retrieve messages when you're away from home. Then make sure you call it frequently. Hourly is a good idea. There are touch tone pay phones all over Chicago. Keep change handy or use a calling card.

A beeper is indispensable. If you get only one job because you got the call immediately, you'll have paid for it. Keep it with you. Keep it on.

Mobile phones and car phones are more expensive but are also useful for keeping in touch with your agent. Make sure your agent has all your numbers. Leave those numbers on your answering machine. Add those numbers to your home number when you sign in at auditions. A casting director may need to contact you when your agent's office is closed. Shop around. You can find some very good deals on beepers in Chicago.

Many people, in addition to answering machines, pagers and mobile phones, will use an answering service. Many people in Chicago have used Talent Connection for years. There are others. You'll find their ads in the Chicago trade papers. Ask for references.

Whatever means you choose, use it. An answering machine does no good if it's not on or checked. A beeper does no good if no one has the number. Common sense.

Why would I need a map?

Again, common sense. You need to know the quickest, safest route to the audition or booking.

If you are new to Chicago, ask a longtime resident to show you around. Use a map during the tour to check where you are and how you got there. Even if you've lived here all your life, as I have, there will still be areas of which you are uncertain. A good map is indispensable.

Most of the agents are located between North Avenue and the Chicago River. The same holds true for casting directors and their casting venues. Most recording studios are also in the vicinity as are the ad agencies.

Theatres are all over the city and suburbs. So are the locations for film and commercial shoots.

Parking can be a problem and while everyone understands if your parking karma fails you occasionally, it is not an acceptable reason for being late. Many casting directors have lateness perimeters and will refuse to see you if you go beyond them. Allow for lack of parking as well as traffic. In the summer, plan your route well to avoid running into road repair. In Chicago there are two seasons, Winter and Construction.

The well-known deficiencies of Chicago public transport are universally bemoaned, but, again, not a sufficient excuse for lateness. While it is well to travel by train or bus, you need to leave plenty of time for delays. Learn the various CTA routes and stock up on tokens. You can get just about anywhere in town on public transport.

Just what kind of wardrobe will I need?

Theatre auditions are different from on-camera auditions. Generally you can audition in comfortable clothes that flatter you and give you room to move. You may want to suggest a character but don't go overboard. On the other hand, dress appropriately for the play. Women should wear a longer skirt for Shakespeare and other period productions. I, personally, wouldn't read for a Sam Shepard cowboy while sporting a three-piece suit.

What you wear to an on-camera audition depends on the roles

you are seeking. Before you go shopping, figure out what you will probably be called for. Then discuss this with your agent. Watch network TV for hairstyles and clothing. Make notes. Then go shopping.

If you can't afford to back up a truck to Bloomingdales (and who of us can), haunt the sales and the outlets. If you are booked on a commercial you can often buy the clothes used in the shoot for half price. Consignment stores will offer almost brand new clothes for a fraction of their original cost. And then there are the actors' happy clothes-hunting grounds- the resale and thrift stores.

This is not just for grunge and bag lady costumes. Oh, no. You can find some amazing bargains in the better resale shops. Be ready to go often and to watch for their sales. You can pick up several whole outfits for peanuts when you happen on a "bag sale" or "dollar days." Many resale shops benefit organizations supported by people with great taste and even bigger checkbooks.

How many looks will I need?

You will probably need casual, dress and business looks. There is upscale business, as in corporate, then down the ladder to middle management, clerical and blue collar. Be familiar with store and designer styles. A casting director will sometimes send out a call that says "more J. Crew than Gap," or "the women are Laura Ashley, the men L.L. Bean."

Some actors keep "character" clothes in their wardrobes. Do this only if you generally get calls for such: nerdy shirts with pocket protectors, Mardi Gras glasses, June Cleaver shirtwaists and aprons, bowling shirts.... You get the drift. Some actors will also invest in hard-hats, doctor coats, nurse uniforms, pharmacists smocks and more. You will be told that these are not mandatory but you may want to have them to bring along just in case. The casting directors have imaginations, the clients don't always.

The most important thing about wardrobe is that you have it

clean and ready at a moment's notice. Try to keep clothes in your closet just for auditions. And have options. If you get booked you will have to bring wardrobe choices to the shoot.

What is an ear prompter and do I really need one?

An ear prompter is a device which allows the actor to recite complicated technical data or an involved business script with seeming ease. The actor reads his lines into a small tape recorder which can be hidden in his pocket. Then in the audition or the filming he plays back the recording. A small wire runs from the recorder to an earpiece and the actor hears the lines and repeats them.

There are several schools, such as Act One Studios, at which you can be trained to operate an ear prompter. Once you are proficient, you may note it under "special skills" on your resume. Make sure your agent knows.

Once again, this is only for industrials. Don't bother with the expense if you have no interest in doing industrials.

A word of caution. Casting directors in Chicago have warned actors against using the ear at auditions for commercials or less dense industrial scripts. They report that it is impossible to direct actors when their performance has already been recorded. You may be precise, but you sure aren't spontaneous.

Anything else?

Yes, self knowledge. This is less tangible than a cellular phone or a tape but indispensable. In fact, if you lacke this, the others are useless. This is tha hardest thing for an actor sometimes. You must know who you are and where you fit in the market. "Typing" yourself for commercial work is a stinky job but you must do it before you try to market yourself. WatchTV (the shows and commercials), films and theatre. See who is doing what, selling what, being hored for what. Whom are you like.

Nothing is set in stone here and tastes do change but see what is out there that you could realistically get. There are certain looks hired for certain markets. If you are overweight you're not likely going to be the McDonald's mom. This is tough stuff but this is a tough business. The look is everything. Be consoled: I doubt, brilliant as he was, that Sir Laurence Olivier would have booked a Bud Lite spot.

AUDITIONING

What is the one thing an actor absolutely, possitively must do in an audition?

LISTEN. Listen to your agent's direction. Listen to the casting director and the director's words. You cannot listen if you are busy agreeing (or, worse, disagreeing) with them or talking to other actors. Just be quiet and listen.

How does the commercial audition process start?

The audition process for a commercial starts with a call from your agent saying "I have an audition for you." She will then tell you where it is, what time you are scheduled for, what the product or who the client is, what the look is, if there are sides when they are available and what are the shoot dates. Make sure that you get all this information. Leave the questions and comments about anything else out of the conversation until you have cleared up this matter.

Once she has given you the information, repeat it back to her to make sure that there is no misunderstanding. Ask about conflicts. Find out when you can pick up the copy if she has it or if she could fax it to you. You may also need to ask if the casting director is asking for more than one picture and resume. It should be your rule to always to carry several copies of your headshot and resume (and your voice-over tape) with you whenever you leave the house.

What happens if I'm not home when the agent calls and I do not have a beeper?

You must make it a rule to call your answering machine or service EVERY HOUR. Auditions sometimes come in at the last minute. For this reason it is also wise to keep your hair clean and make-up or a razor (whichever your gender requires) with you at all times. A client might be able to look past inappropriate clothing but a scruffy appearance is off-putting and lack of pictures is unprofessional.

As soon as you get a message from your agent, fly to the phone and check in. Even before returning the call from your mother. Having talked to your agent before your mother insures that you can then tell Mom you just spoke to your agent. You then have an excuse to get off the phone when she starts asking if you're eating well by saying you have to prepare for an audition.

Joking aside, you must check for messages hourly and return all calls from your agent. Calling an agent back to verify that you are going to be at the audition is called confirming. Many casting directors will drop you from the audition list if your agent cannot confirm you by a certain time.

Keep your appointment book with you and record all the information. When you're out of work and collective unemployment you can use this information to fill out those where-I-went-to-look-for-work forms.

What if I'm multi-listed and more than one agent calls me for the same audition?

It's simple. You take the audition from the one who called you first. Don't play games.

And remember to budget at least one hour for each audition and to factor in travel time when you are scheduling more than one audition (lucky you) in a day.

How can I prepare for a commercial audition?

Get the copy if you can, and memorize it. Read any directions and follow them. Dress appropriately. Then leave plenty of time to get there about ten to fifteen minutes early.

Re-read the above paragraph. Then read on.

You may not be able to get the copy. If you do, be prepared for it to be completely changed when you get to the audition. Also be prepared for the fact that the character description may change. You may even be asked to read for another character. I've been called for a United Nations delegate, read for a nurse and cast as a mom all on the same commercial.

As for getting there on time, assume there will be no parking or that the train will be stuck at Belmont. Don't let it throw you. Don't let anything throw you. Assume it will all be changed and accept it. Then do your very best job.

What do I do when I get there?

Do not arrive too early. Yes, I know I just said assume that you're going to be held up at least fifteen minutes. If you get there too early, go have a cup of coffee. Decaf is a good bet. Then show up your standard ten to fifteen early.

What if you are running late? If you think you are going to be even five minutes behind, take a moment to call your agent and ask her to call the casting director. This can happen if you have auditions back to back and the first one runs long, if the client's plane was stuck in Des Moines or he can't figure out where he wants to go to dinner. Phone first.

The audition process sounds like a mess.

Anything that can go wrong will. You know it. Your agent knows it. The casting director knows it. The only one who hasn't caught on is the client. And guess who it is you have to shine for? That's right, the suits. So handle everything. Be calm. Don't let it get to you. And do your job. Sometimes it's the hardest thing you'll have to do.

What about make-up for auditions?

Women should be familiar with good camera make-up and how to modify it for a particular role. Women should always wear a base when going before a camera. Just assume that the audition will be taped. And many casting directors suggest that men, especially those with pale or very fair skin, also wear some kind of base.

While on the subject of skin, stay out of the sun, especially if you burn. A sunburn will keep you out of an audition as well as ruin your skin. This is the Midwest. Commercials here don't run to fun in the sun on the beach. So deep tans are out as well. When you get to the audition don't waste your time schmoozing with pals or scoping out the competition. Don't stand around talking loudly and laughing more loudly. The casting directors hate it. Sound carries and they can't tape. Other actors hate it because they can't concentrate. The casting directors, of course, are the ones who have the power not to call you in again. Whomever you choose not to offend, don't gab. Tell your pals you'll meet them for coffee afterwards.

So, I should just mind my own business, is that it?

Sure, but don't lower the energy in the room. There are actors who can change the feel of a whole room just by walking in with their gloom, greed or insecurity. I've known the temperature of a room to drop a good twenty degrees whenever one particular actress entered. She was cold and determined and never shared the camaraderie of the rest of us. There we were helping each other by pooling the information we had, the cuts, the changes, the directions, sharing the script if necessary and she wanted no part of it.

Other actors carry a cloud of gloom with them just like the little man in the comics. It, too, is contagious and unwanted. These actors will often wonder why they are not called in and why they seldom are booked. It's tough work for an agent to tell an actor that he's a bummer.

Instead of invading other actors' space, put your stuff down (and in Chicago winters this can be a major undertaking). Get out your pictures and resumes. Go find the sign-in sheet and fill it out completely. Fill out all the forms- and there may well be several. Most casting offices will post a notice over the sign-in table giving you instructions. Follow them. Double check. Indicate on the form (if it calls for it) if you are willing to work as an extra. And then stand by your decision. Saying you will work as an extra does not mean that it takes you out of consideration as a principal.

Don't waste your time and get your knickers in a twist flipping back through the sign-in sheet to see who was called in among your heavy competition. Negative activity messes you up. Just take care of you.

Be sure to check conflicts; both product and shoot dates. They may, like everything else, have changed. Check when the callbacks are scheduled.

What if I'm in a play and there are performances and rehearsals? Are those conflicts?

Check the form if you need a theatre release.

A theatre release means that you must be released from the shoot at a certain time if you have a theatre commitment. This includes the time you need to get to the theatre for half-hour (the 30 minute call prior to curtain most Equity houses require). It doesn't include having tickets to *Les Miserables*- no matter how much they cost.

You will be asked to fill out a size card. Don't put down the size you hope to be. Be honest. If you are cast, this is what the wardrobe folks will work from. And won't you look silly when they bring in a size four that will never make it over those hips?

Each casting director's form is a bit different. Make sure you fill out everything you should. Make sure your phone number(s) are where they should be on the forms. Sometimes there is last minute late night casting long after the agents are home in bed. You want the job? Let them know how to find you.

What happens after I fill out all the forms; just wait?

You will most likely be asked to make a slate. A slate is generally a piece of paper on which you write your name and, sometimes, your agent. Some casting offices actually use chalk slates. And some casting offices will have the slates already made up for you. On the rare call, you will have no paper slate and you will just say your name and (possibly) agent to the camera when you audition. Some voice over auditions do not use names at all but give each actor a number. Keep your slate with you. You will hold it under your chin when you begin your audition. The casting director or her assistant may take a Polaroid of you. These Polaroids will help the director or client remember what you looked like that day- not what your headshot says you look like. Unlike headshots, Polaroids are hideously lit, heartlessly cruel and cannot be airbrushed. They invariably look dreadful. But, guess what, the casting director knows that and does not need to be reminded by your whining. So shut up about it and staple it to your cards if you are so instructed. Lately some casting directors have been using a new camera that shoots a picture from the video monitor. The results are much more flattering.

Will I be given directions about how to play the character?

Find the copy (what you say) and learn it. Read all the copy, not just your lines. Read the left hand side of the page where the directions are written. Figure out what they want.

Some commercials are MOS - "Mit out sound"- you guessed it, German. It means the actors don't talk. In this case either you will just rely on looks or you will make up your own dialogue which will not be heard on the finished spot.

In some commercials you will be asked to improvise everything. Here training pays off. Some actors hate this. Others revel in it. Here, too, a dumb partner can kill you. But only if you let them - be prepared to caryy it completely by yourself if neccessary. Don't be pushy and carry it by yourself if you don't have to.

SAG gas a specific policy regarding improvising on an audition. "If a principal performer is to be required to improvise during an audition, he/she shall be so advised prior to the audition. When principal performer is required to improvise during an audition, such audition shall be deemed an ad lib or creative session call from the inception of such audition call and the principal performer shall be paid for such services as set forth..." Should you be asked to ad lib, go ahead. Don't compromise your audition. But then call your agent immediately and report this. You may also call the SAG office to see if what you were asked to do qualifies as "improvising" and if you are entitled to compensation.

Often there will be story boards on the wall to show you what the commercial or industrial will look like. If you've never seen one, they look similar to comic strip frames. They show the visual part of the commercial. Also, there will often be instructions about the characters and action. Read and remember. Pay strict attention to what they want.

Many times, too, the casting director will come out and tell you specific directions about the project. She will tell you what the clients are looking for and what they want to avoid. Typically a casting director will say "They want this very real. Real people. No acting." That will mean just that, do it very low key, like those slice-of-life commercials. Do it well. They, the clients, can always get real people if they want. And for a whole lot less money. In point of fact, that's what is happening a great deal lately. So preserve your job. Be real. Simple. If that's what is called for.

On the other hand the casting director may come out and say that they want something really wacky. She may give a character or actor on TV as an example. Those mind-numbing hours of watching network TV may just pan out. Listen and do as she says.

She may also give some more specific directions such as a change in the script, a cut or a shift in camera angles. Again pay attention and remember when you go into the audition. Casting directors become justifiably irate when they have explained things out in the lobby to a sea of bobbing actor heads only to have those same actors suffer sudden and total amnesia when they come before the client. It makes everybody look bad.

While waiting, study your lines. Learn them. Be prepared with a number of readings. And don't set anything in stone. They may ask for something else. Don't be constipated by your own choices.

You may well be matched with other actors if you are being seen in groups. Pay attention when the groups are called out. Then go and rehearse with your partner(s).

What if I loathe the person with whom I am paired?

If you know the casting director well enough, you may ask to be switched. She may be able to accommodate you. Don't ask often or you will get the reputation for being difficult. If you are stuck with El Stinko, make the best of it. You are an actor after all.

What will I do in the actual audition?

Be ready with your slate, picture, resume and all your forms. When you are called, go into the taping calm and assured because you are prepared. (That is what you've been doing out there isn't it? Preparing instead of posturing and pretending for the other actors.)

Be calm. Never panic. Never let anyone know you don't have a dime and this job is all that stands between you and a cardboard box on Lower Wacker Drive. Again, remember you are an actor. Don't smarm either. Be pleasant and business-like.

When you go into the taping room it may be just you and the casting director, maybe her assistant, or you, another actor and the casting director, or the director may be there or the client or any combination thereof. Don't forget to be polite to the human being who is working the camera. If the director or client offers to shake hands do so. Don't initiate the gesture. If they are (and in some cases they will be) rude, surly or stupid, don't feel obliged to point it out to them. Just let it go. Do your job as well as you know you can no matter what the circumstances and leave graciously.

Follow whatever directions you are given. These may be confusing or obscure or completely opposite to what you had prepared. Sort out what is being asked of you, change where you can. Sometimes there are hidden agendas going on between client and the director. It's your job to divine what it is they want from you even if they can't articulate it. This is close to impossible but it is part of your job. For the most part the process runs very smoothly and everyone is pleasant and articulate.

What if the commercial turns out to be objectionable to me on moral, religious or political grounds?

If you have strong views about products or companies you will not do commercials, for let your agent know. Then don't go on the call. There are actors who will not do ads for certain products or organizations. I am one. But that is between me and my agent.

But what if you get to the audition and find an ugly surprise? Suppose the copy is gay-bashing, demeaning to women or a minority or has a religious slate you cannot support. Don't get hysterical or incensed publicly. Explain to the casting director that you may have a conflict, you need not explain what. Call your agent immediately and explain calmly the situation. Follow her advice. If you need to leave, explain calmly. Don't take it out on the casting director.

And in the case of just stupid copy?

If you hate it and you don't care about the job, then leave. You may well incur the wrath of your agent and never be called in by that casting director again but if you feel that strongly, go ahead. If you don't feel that strongly, say the copy. Don't, as I have seen, instruct the director or client as to how much better it would be if they used your version. You want to be a copywriter or an actor? Yes, we all know some of it is dreadful but making it sound good is part of our job.

Where do I stand and what do I look at?

You will be told which camera to look at or where to stand. The casting director may have made a mark, often a tee-shape, on the floor. This is called your mark. You are to hit it and stay there. The camera is focused to that mark. So if you want your face on camera...

You may be told to play to the camera as if it were the other person, even if you are reading with another actor. You may be asked to cheat out when playing to the other characters. This means that you keep your face as much to camera as possible.

This commercial may be what is called a "Bite And Smile." You've seen them on TV. You take a bite and react. If this is a Bite And Smile, there will be a spit bucket handy. You do not have to swallow whatever it is you are tasting. You may, when the cameras stop rolling, spit it out discreetly. Ted Hoerl of Rabedeau Casting has some pithy rules for a Bite And Smile. They include not being shocked that it actually tastes good and that nothing exploded in your mouth so nothing needs explode on your face.

If you are asked to do the scene again, listen to the direction and adapt. Say thank you when they do, and leave.

Then what do I do?

Here comes a really hard part. After you have called your agent to tell her how it went, FORGET IT. Difficult, I know, but vital for your very survival. Don't dwell on it even if it is a national spot which will run on every network in perpetuity. Let it go. Be pleasantly surprised if you get a callback. If you get feedback from your agent, listen to it. But try to let go.

What do I do if I get a callback?

First of all don't spend money as if you actually had booked the job. That is rule number one.

Rule number two is to stay cool. It is generally accepted that you wear to the callback what you wore to the audition, unless you've been told otherwise. It's also not a good idea to shave your head, dye your hair or get a tattoo before the callback. They liked you as you were. That's an overly dramatic way of saying don't change anything. No serious haircuts. A trim is okay.

Follow the same rules as you did before. Be prepared. (Actually, come to think of it, acting does have a lot in common with Scouting.) As before, assume that everything you've been told may change in a heartbeat and be ready to adapt. You may show up ready to repeat your stellar audition as the chef only to find that, brilliant as your chef was, you're being considered for the lobster.

Don't panic when you see who else is called back. Competition can be very intimidating. Don't waste energy second-guessing the director.

There may very well be rewrites of the copy. Don't be stuck in a mindset of "But yesterday I...." You may have a different partner. You may be tried in several different groups. You may be asked to stay. You may be dismissed immediately after you have read.

As before, just do your very best job, and be pleasant and get out, call your agent and then forget about it. With film and commercials the look is everything. You may have been perfect. Your reading, even of abysmal copy, may have been perfect. Your taking of direction, even from a monosyllabic advertising account head who was in open warfare with the loudmouth client, may have been perfect. But if someone looked more like the parent of the only three-year-old actor they could get who could do a somersault, eat a waffle and cry on cue, guess what, he got it. Your turn is coming.

TRAINING

What kinds of classes are offered in Chicago?

Just about everything.

There are on-camera classes for film, TV and commercials. There are classes to learn to use the ear prompter. You can study cold reading. You can work on scene study, monologues and audition techniques. There are improvisation classes as well as classes in voice-overs, voice, singing, dancing, directing, playwriting and more.

What do I need?

That very much depends on what you already know and what you want to do. If you have no desire to ever appear before a camera, there is no need for on-camera work or learning the ear prompter. If you have a basic knowledge of on-camera technique and really want to make the big bucks pushing toothpaste, an intermediate level commercial technique class would be a good idea.

Directors will look at your resume for your training. They want to know what you've learned, where you learned it and who taught it to you. It gives them some reference. This is especially important for actors just starting out. Later the director will look at your credits. But for now, when credits are few or mainly from college productions, the training section of your resume is very important.

Stage work demands training. Voice and movement classes are needed just as much as scene study, a fact often overlooked by student actors. Improvisation is a big help but is not in itself sufficient training to qualify you as an actor. This is a tough business, you have to have built up some muscles. Stage combat and juggling and the like are nice accessories. You never know when they will come in handy.

If you want to work in musicals or in plays with dance or singing, you need to have trained in these disciplines and continue to exercise. In the same vein, actors who also do straight plays will want to keep their skills sharp and to learn new skills.

What are the advantages of taking classes in Chicago if I already have training elsewhere?

Good question. In the first place, you can fill in the gaps and expand your knowledge while keeping fresh between jobs (yes, that can happen).

In the second place, you will be doing the training IN CHICAGO where Chicago casting types can see your work and where you can work with other actors. Many actors are also directors or playwrights. There is a new theatre company springing up every week. Just as in any other business, theatre in Chicago relies heavily on networking. Taking a GOOD class in Chicago will put you in touch with other actors, directors and playwrights. This contact may well lead to auditions, roles, companies and the foundation of a career. That is not to say that if you sign up for a class you will automatically be propelled to stardom. But, on the other hand, you're not going to meet anyone sitting home watching the Shopping Network.

You said a GOOD class. What's a good class?

One that teaches you what you need to know and exercises your skills on the appropriate level. You will be bored senseless in a beginners class if you are further advanced, just as you will be overwhelmed and discouraged if you are tackling Chekhovian inner monologues when you haven't a clue where are up and downstage. For most good classes you need to interview or audition.

A good class is also one taught by a positive, fair, professional teacher who knows the material and knows how to get the message across. This excludes the disappointed whiners, the psychotic, the egomaniacal, the terminally out-of-touch and the fundamentally incompetent.

Now that you are terrified to put down money anywhere for fear of being lumbered with one of these, here's how to avoid that. Check the credentials, both of the establishment and of the teacher. Ask other actors you know. This is a good way to weed out the weird but it does not guarantee that you'll have a merry romp. Some teachers and some actors just do not agree. I've known three students to take exactly the same class and one loved the teacher, one loathed him and the last was indifferent. It's chemistry.

You will do well to stay with the established firms, the better theatres. By established, I don't necessarily mean longest with their shingle out. There are some that have been around donkey's years and are either rip-offs, light years out-of-touch or not the place for you. The ones with the biggest ads and the largest selection of classes are not necessarily the best either. Ask around. Ask your agent. That's always a good idea.

Some establishments offer a smorgasbord of classes. You can take one or a number, depending on your needs. Some, on the other hand, have a structured curriculum and one class builds upon another. Figure out what suits you.

Should I take a class with a director or casting director just so she gets to know me?

Well, isn't that a thorny question! There is much discussion in Chicago about casting directors who also teach. There are a fair few who do. Some folks are violently against the idea and level charges of conflict of interest, subtle coercion etc. Others believe it's a good way for actors to learn just what is expected of them. Like it or not, it is a fact of life here. You can choose to take a casting director's classes or not. Take them only if she is teaching what you need to know, otherwise be aware that you are spending money in a blatant attempt to be noticed. If that sits with you, so be it. Whether you study with a casting director or learn from some other competent teacher, learn. You will benefit enormously from learning as much as possible about every aspect of the business.

Where do I find out about classes?

A copy of The Actor's Training Guide or PerformInk Newspaper will get you started. Ask around. Many places have fliers. Ask your agent, or actors whose work you admire. If you have liked a particular director's work, call the theatre and see if and where she teaches.

What about workshops?

Weekend seminars or one- or two-meeting workshops are frequently offered. They are, for the most part, valuable. The more you know, the better off you are. Knowledge is power.

The information you hear one place may be totally discounted in the next place. But that's the same all over. One agent may love your headshot, the next thinks it fit only to line the parrot's cage. You have to do a lot of processing.

SAG and AFTRA offer workshops, as do some theatres and training centers. The SAG and AFTRA workshops are open, for the most part, to non-members. PerformInk and National Photo have, in the past, sponsored audition clinics. PerformInk is also a good source for finding out about other upcoming programs.

Every other year Chicago hosts an International Theatre Festival and the visiting artists often share their knowledge. From time to time teachers who travel the country stop in Chicago. Their arrivals and schedules will be in publications like PerformInk, Screen Magazine, Chicago Filmletter and Audition News.

What about taking classes at a college or university? Chicago is known for its training programs.

Not possible, alas. You can take classes if you are enrolled at the university. You cannot take just one class on an occasional basis. There's always a chance you may want to go back to finish up or pursue a higher degree. But, as of now, you cannot just drop in at Northwestern to brush up your Shakespeare.

One last word about classes. Modeling schools are for models. Acting schools are for actors. What is it you want to be? Decide that and then go where the best teachers are. And never even think about signing with an agent who insists that you first take her classes. That will be your first clue she is not legitimate. Chicago agents may participate in seminars from time to time, but no real agency offers classes. That bit of information should save you heartache, anger and several hundred dollars.

What about private coaches?

As one who teaches at the university level and also coaches privately, I say a private coach is good for some things and not a good idea for others. For instance? If you are just starting in the business and have never been in a group class, a private coach is not the place to begin. There is a special energy and dynamic that happens in a good beginning acting class that you cannot get one-on-one. You can learn a great deal by watching others who are learning the basics as well.

Certainly improvisation is best in a group. Scene study, unless you and a partner want private coaching, demands greater numbers. The decision is basic and logical. You cannot teach directing without bodies to direct.

Having said that, there are times when a private coach is an enormous help. No one should ever audition with a monologue which has not been coached. You absolutely need another pair of eyes. An audition coach can be invaluable. If you don't choose to hire a professional coach, a fellow actor or a director friend can help if they are objective and constructive. It makes galaxies of difference.

Why? Because a coach (be he a friend or teacher) will make you do the work you might let slide. Because a private coach can see the effect you are creating, which is often world's apart from the intention. He can give hints to jump start a piece, to retool and revitalize a piece that is growing stale. He can tell you which audition piece is appropriate for a given situation (different theatres, agents...) He may even help you find new pieces that will replace, be a compliment to or contrast with your current repertoire.

It is as important to have your audition monologue well coached as it is to have it well chosen and well rehearsed. Good coaching (wherever it comes from) is as important as a good picture and resume.

This is true for auditions in which you are asked to bring in three minutes or so of your choice. General auditions fall in this category. They call for a monologue, sometimes two. These need to be well coached. Additionally many actors will come to their coaches when they have been given material to learn for an initial or call-back audition.

A coach can also help with scene work, but be careful. Hiring a coach to work with you when you are not getting what you feel you need from a director in a production can be very dicey. That's a difficult call but if you feel desperately in need of help, give it a try.

Some actors will choose to work with a private coach when studying camera work or cold reading. This can work well, but so can working in a group to learn on-camera techniques. It's your call. One affords you intense individual attention, the other the chance to observe.

A private coach is also useful for learning a dialect, either for an audition, a production or just to have against a time when you may need it.

Many actors use a coach either primarily or in the course of other work. They may be used to help find direction in your career. This can be especially helpful for actors new to Chicago or to the business.

Singers swear by a vocal coach.

How do I pick the class or coach that is right for me?

Just the same way you date- or choose an agent, therapist, doctor or roommate. Be well informed. Know who is out there and how they work. Ask around. Call the coach and talk with him or her. You'll know almost immediately if this is a good match. Ask the theatre for the brochure, or to sit in on a class. Ask someone who has studied with the teacher. Better idea- ask several people so you can get a consensus. Before you plunk down the cash, find out about refunds if you get cast in a show or have a major conflict once he class begins.

If you sign up and discover you hate it; ask yourself why. Is it the teacher? Is she not good or is she daring to point out failings in your work which you would much rather ignore? Are you in a class the level which does not match your experience? Perhaps you should drop the class, or perhaps you should tough it out and learn something- because there is always something to be learned, no matter how grim the experience. In this business you find you are given truckloads of lemons. Early on find a whizbang recipe for lemonade.

Do I list training on my resume?

You bet. As I mentioned earlier, people will want to know "who stamped your card." List your training under, appropriately, "Training." If you have a teacher of international renown, list him or her first. To save egos and perhaps an ugly scene, I've found it prudent to list the rest of your training in alphabetical order.

The advantage of listing your training is that it says that you know what you are doing. It affords a chance for them to start conversations such as, "Oh, I see you worked with Arabella Raffleflap. Does she still spit at students?" And it fills up the resume when the credits are scarce.

You can market the knowledge you gain in classes and coaching sessions in the "Special Skills" section. If you've studied voice, dance, combat, juggling, dialects, etc., list them there. Along with your other shining talents such as fluent Sanskrit and large animal husbandry.

So you think I ought to study?

Yes. It's something you need right after breath and love. But like those other two, only if the source is good. As an actor you need to keep growing, pushing yourself and presenting yourself to new surroundings. This town is about adapting, growing and networking.

A footnote: Take the time to also learn other things, not just those directly related to the business. A class in a foreign language will open you to new ways of thinking, will give you insight into another culture. Yes, it will look good on the resume, but it also keeps your mind sharp. Additionally, it keeps your mind for a moment off this business. We can grow myopic, obsessed and depressed.

If theatre or acting is all you learn, then theatre and acting is all you know. And if theatre is all you know, then theatre is all you are. That's not ideal even when things are going swimmingly; when agents and directors are cueing up to pay you huge compliments and big money.

Be more than an acting wonk. We laugh at the nerds with their high pants, slide rules, Scotch-taped glasses and pocket protectors. The ones who know nothing but quarks, logarithms and other things that make me break out in hives. But what if we are theatre nerds? Get out of the green room and the studio. Take a class. Get a life.

PART TWO:
WHERE THE WORK IS

FILM & TELEVISION

Are there a lot of movies made in Chicago?

A lot more now than there were twenty years ago. During the reign of the first Mayor Daley there were no films made here. Perhaps three. Why? Because Hizzoner didn't want them and whatever Hizzoner wanted or didn't want... You may remember the 1968 Democrat Convention...

That was then. We have a new Mayor Daley and he's all for films. There is an Illinois Film Office and a Chicago Film Office. They work hard to bring pictures to Illinois and to make everything run smoothly once they are here. They do a terrific job.

How do I get in one?

I presume you mean without having to buy a ticket.

Let's start with major motion pictures filming in Chicago. The scenario runs something like this. Before shooting begins, a studio or director will either send out a casting director to Chicago or hire a Chicago casting director- or a combination of both. That is to say, the studio may hire a Chicago casting director to assist the Hollywood type.

Agents are sent the breakdowns of the roles being cast. They may submit actors or the casting directors may make requests- or, again, a combination of both. You are not going to get any work above extra level without an agent.

Your agent will arrange the audition, giving you the time, the place and the look. You should also get the sides. Memorize them. You want to be able to play the scene as fully as possible so memorize the lines.

You will go to the Chicago casting director's office, the production office or sometimes to a hotel room rented by the casting director. You'll sign in. When called, you'll present your picture and resume. Though they will likely already have one picture and resume it's a good idea to bring a couple of copies along. You may chat with the casting director and then you will read (i.e., play the scene). You may be taped. Listen to and follow any direction. When the audition is over, thank them and leave. Report to your agent how it went and then forget about it.

If you get a callback, great. You may not be called back for the same role for which you initially read. Repeat the process. At the callback you may well be reading for the director. Do what he asks. Thank him and leave. Report back to your agent and don't stew about it. As with so many other aspects of this business, the reasons you do or do not get a part are often beyond you

What kinds of films and TV shows are shot here?

There are big films from major studios with big starts. *The Fugitive* is an example. There are smaller films also from big studios. John Hughes shoots almost everything here. Andy Davis comes home to work as often as possible. Oprah Winfrey's Harpo Studios are here and have made two films. Movies-of-the-week and mini-series are shot here too and we've had a few series. Recently "Missing Persons" and "The Untouchables" were both shot here. These are the big guys.

Then there are independent films and student films. In some cases you need to be very careful here. Work closely with your agent. For the most part these films are on the up and up but there are some sleazoids out there. You need to check everything and everyone out with your agent or the union and Illinois Film office. If you don't like the way things are going, if something is fishy or uncomfortable, ask questions. There are some opportunistic people out there trying to exploit your dreams.

Here are a few simple rules to avoid trouble. You never have to pay anyone to be part of a film. You should never have to strip at an audition. No one is allowed to touch you or make provocative remarks. You don't need that or them. Blow the whistle. If you think you are being exploited, lied to, abused or harassed you probably are. Do something about it. Start with your agent.

Don't think that these kinds of lowlife are all over. The majority of the business is well regulated. But I have heard horror stories. This is why we have unions. And if you are going to be serious about films, you would be very wise to join.

For what kinds of roles will I be reading?

First of all, you may read for a film that is not shot in Chicago. Huh? Your agent should get breakdowns for films that are shooting all across the country. She may very well submit you for one of these. You may be taped and the tape sent out to "the coast"- since we're talking about film people, we might as well talk like film people. If you hear of a project and you know exactly what part you would like to be considered for, ask you agent. It's her job to bring you to the director's attention. But be realistic.

The same thing goes for films that are shot in Chicago. If this is a major motion picture, you probably won't be reading for the lead. Or even the second lead. No sooner have I written that then exceptions come to mind. There are cases in which unknown Chicago actors landed leading roles but these, like little Mason Gamble who was found in a nationwide search for Dennis The Menace, are the once-in-a-blue-moon brand of exception.

Sometimes casting directors will conduct a nationwide search for a role. More often than not this is for children or young people. When a major feature is being shot in Chicago, the majority of the roles cast here are the much smaller ones, day players and weekly contracts.

Why? Because to get the foreign distribution and the video business (the two elements, I am told, that truly determine a film's success) Hollywood has to book stars and several of them. Then the stars will want their friends around them. On some pictures, the major stars get to fill a certain number of day player roles and some who have family here get to cast family members. Chicago actors are very lucky to get large roles in films shot here. It happens frequently. There are nice, juicy minor roles that will work throughout the picture. But there is a lot more of the day player variety cast here.

That is not to disparage the work. We are delighted with day player work. With some directors who are notorious for changing their minds and rewriting, a day player can work for weeks.

What's a day player role?

It's the doctor that appears only in a scene or two. The witness who is questioned for two minutes. The guy on the bus who tells Jessica Lange, "He went that way." The waitress who wants to know how Harrison Ford wants his eggs. You are booked for a day or two. A larger role will earn you a weekly contract. If you hit the jackpot, you get a run of the picture deal. These terms are self-explanatory.

What do I do if I get the part?

Besides calling your mother, your high school drama teacher and anyone who ever doubted you? You pick up the sides from your agent or from the production office. Your agent will have negotiated your salary but you probably won't sign the contract until you are on the set.

Wardrobe will call you for a fitting. You will be given some sort of schedule at some time which will probably be changed a couple of times. Movies are like that.

Once you get there you will be sent to the make-up trailer, shown to your trailer, the same routine as in a commercial (see that chapter). The same rules apply. Hurry up and wait and the crew eats first. The food, which is generally very good on commercials, will be even better (one of the many reasons I love making movies).

Do your job. Show up. Rehearse when asked and know your lines. Don't bump into anything, unless it's in the script. Be professional. This precludes asking the star for her autograph or taking anything as a souvenir.

Sounds easy. Is it?

It is not easy. Film acting is very different from working on the stage. You will have heard that and worked on it in an on-camera class but until you've had to play a scene over and over and concentrate in the midst of chaos you really don't have a clue. "If you can keep your head while all about you....." You will also look at movies differently after you've been in a few. Some of the magic is lost but in its place is respect and awe for what has been accomplished.

At the end of your shoot, do as you would on any shoot. Return the clothes - and hang them up even if they are going to be cleaned or discarded. Check out. Get your copy of the contract. Get your call for the next day, if you're lucky enough to be working again. Report your hours to your agent. Go home and write your Oscar acceptance speech.

What about TV?

It will rot your brain.

You mean acting on TV. The procedure is much the same as with feature film. And if you're not dead at the end of the episode there is always the chance you'll reappear.

Chicago has had a few series' shot here but it is not known as a big television town. Lots of series' are set here but very, very few actually shoot here.

Apart from series and movies of the week, there are a handful of children's shows produced locally and some cable efforts. Cable is tricky because much of that work is non-union. As with any non-union work, you need to research the project and the principals very well.

The rest of the Chicago-based television is chat shows, news and public affairs. Very rarely does one of the stations produce an original script, but anything can happen. If a project is new or unknown, ask questions. It's easier to get out of a difficult situation early.

Occasionally a show such as "America's Most Wanted" will shoot in Chicago. Then a director will come out here and cast through one of the casting agents. The procedure is the same. Know what you're reading for, show up, sign in, know your lines, do a good job and leave it behind you. Often they are looking for people who resemble the subjects in the actual case.

What about any soap operas?

None in Chicago, except maybe on cable. The soap operas in New York and Los Angeles will sometimes send out a call. Agents will tape the actors whom they feel are appropriate for the open roles. Good luck.

What is pilot season?

This is the time of year when all the networks and producers are lining their new television shows for test runs. They shoot the pilot, the first episode; sometimes that's as long as a show lasts, others go on to run for years.

The calls will go out to Chicago from the coast for roles in upcoming shows. These will either come through a casting director or directly to your agent. You will be taped and the tape sent to the producer. Chicago actors have actually landed roles in a series this way.

Just because there isn't a great deal of television produced in Chicago doesn't mean Chicago actors don't get a crack at what's going on across the country.

What about film extra work?

There are currently two casting directors for film extra work and they are always busy. Film extra work has all of the drawbacks of film principal work (long hours, uncertain schedules, boredom) and few of the rewards. The pay is generally about 50 dollars a day and you sometimes get a bag lunch while the principals are making a whole lot more and tucking into something a whole bunch tastier. BUT you're in the movie!

The experience is invaluable. You learn what goes on. It's a lot better to view the mayhem from a safe distance, when you don't have to pour out your soul to a churning Speed Graphic's Lens. You learn who does what and who goes where. You'll learn what a half apple is and a dolly. They are not a light fruity snack and a child's plaything.

You can put the experience on your resume. That way if you have no other screen credits, this will tell prospective directors that you do in fact know your way around a film set. It shows you're learning.

And there's a possible bonus. Sometimes an extra can be up-graded. That means you are given a line or two and a moment in front of the camera. That means more money and a chance to join the union. And isn't that what you wanted? Don't, for heaven's sake, go to the set determined to be upgraded. You'll only annoy the crew and director and come away universally loathed. Just do your job and hope that the fates are especially kind that day.

Film extra work can be a great start. You need to send headshots and resumes to the extra casters. Sometimes there are open registrations. Sometimes a call will go out for a specific type or ethnic group. The Act One Reports will have a current listing of the film extra casting offices. Check it out.

What about student films?

This, too, can be a good place to start. These you can put on your resume and you can get copies. You can edit your scenes in these films on to your reel (a videotape of yourself acting) to send to agents and directors. Here you may get a chance to play large roles and get some serious screen time. Columbia College and Art Institute have a very good film departments, and the students are often looking for actors for their thesis projects.

SAG actors can appear in these films if a waiver is signed. The agreement between SAG and the director or film company says that if the film does go on to make money, the union members will be then paid for their services. Again, in good student films, SAG actors get a chance to spend quality time in front of the camera. It's great practice and you improve with practice.

What about independent films?

For the most part, if these are union films, you will be protected against exploitation of most sorts. But even some signatory producers, companies who have an agreement with the union, have run into trouble.

Look at the project carefully. Many are just fine but some are shady. Look carefully at the subject matter. If these are cheap horror or female exploitation films you can pretty much expect horror and exploitation. You'll smell it when you walk in the door. It is your agent's job to protect you from these slimeballs who want to pay you nothing, take you off to the Wisconsin woods and film you being hacked to ribbons all wet and naked and cowering in the shower. Women are especially vulnerable. Young, pretty women. If asked to dinner after the audition, suggest you bring your agent along.

And if you run into any harassment, exploitation or slobberer, report these lowlifes to the union, your agent, the Illinois Film Office and the Illinois Department of Labor. Despite what they may threaten, you will work in this town again. And by the grace of God, they won't.

COMMERCIALS

What kinds of commercials are there?

Commercials which run across the country are called nationals. They are always union jobs. They pay a shooting fee and residuals. Residuals are the fees paid for using your work after the initial run of the commercial. Sometimes commercials can run forever. Lucky you.

Not all commercials are the national spots you see on the networks. Those are the ones we all dream of getting. The ones that will put braces on our kids' teeth and make the down payment on a two flat in a good neighborhood. They are the ones that pay so handsomely and enable us to do theatre which, for the most part, pays so miserably.

Commercials which are shown only in certain areas (the South, the East, etc.) are called regionals. These, too, are union spots. The residual rate is lower.

Most local spots (an ad for the Chicago Tribune or the Chicagoland Dodge dealers) are union as well and pay residuals.

Some spots are shot for a specific time (a President's Day Sale, Christmas, etc.). These will only run for one cycle (time period) and so the residuals will be small. The pay scale is lower for use on cable television.

There are some commercials which are shot for local markets which are non-union. Whereas some of these are very good, some are atrocious. We can all cite examples of embarrassingly bad commercials shot on pathetically low budgets. The kind that use inexperienced actors, often the business owner and far too many members of his extended family.

Be warned that when accepting a non-union commercial you have no guarantee that you will be paid either your session fee or any residuals. Most non-union spots are biy-outs (you are paid for your work but recieve no residuals no matter how long they run the spot).That is not to say that all non-union operations are out to bilk the actors. By no means. You do have recourse to the Department of Labor if you are abused or not paid.

We talked earlier of Bite And Smile. That's short hand for the sort of shot in a commercial where the actor tastes the product and reacts favorably. We've spoken of commercials shooting MOS. There is a school of commercial which some call "Real People" in which the actor is requested to act without looking as though he is actually an actor.

It's simpler than it sounds, but that doesn't mean it's easy. You will recognize these spots. They are generally shot in black and white with a steady-cam. Or they are shot with people meant to be "man on the street" or pseudo-documentary style. Actors need to be very good at these because there is a movement among ad agencies and their clients to hire actual "real people" to shoot these. This takes the bread out of our mouths and reinforces the popular belief that anyone can do what we do.

You may be told that a commercial you are auditioning for is a PSA. That stands for Public Service Announcement. These are ads for The American Lung Association, The United Negro College Fund etc. The fees for these are lower but then, not only do you have the knowledge you are benefiting your fellow man, you can be comforted in knowing that everyone involved is taking a paycut.

How do I know if I got the job?

Your agent will tell you- eventually. This process can take a while. I sometimes think booking a job in Chicago is like being a contestant in The Miss America pageant. They keep whittling down the contestants and at each phase you've got to keep smiling and keep working.

The easiest way to book a commercial or industrial is to go to the audition, go home and have the telephone ring in a short time with your agent on the other line telling you you've got the job and where and when to report. It doesn't often work that simply.

First of all, it may take some time for all the parties involved to see the tape of your audition. Then they have to decide. Some corporate client types have lots of agendas that come into play, the least of which is matching you up with the other characters. Often they will make a "short list," those actors they are interested in but about whom they have made no final decisions. At this point they will call the casting director, who will call your agent to check your availability. A "check avail" is not a booking. Don't spend the money yet. What the call means is that the client is interested in you (as well as others) and is checking to make sure that you are still available the day of the shoot.

They may also say that they are "icing" you for the day(s). This is or is not a firm booking depending on who you ask. This is one of the infuriating ambiguities in the business. This must all be worked out with your agent. Follow her advice. That way if something goes wrong, you are not at fault because you followed her advice.

You may hear nothing else. If the day of the shoot comes and goes, you can pretty well figure you didn't get it. Take the compliment that they were interested enough to check your availability and then move on.

You may hear nothing for a while and then your agent will call to say that you are booked. Hooray. You will need information. Your agent may not yet have it. But you need to get it as soon as she, or someone from the production, can give it to you.

How will I know how much I'm going to make?

Your agent will negotiate your salary whenever possible. The majority of commercials will just pay scale. If you're a "big smell" in Chicago you can negotiate for more. The agent should try to get you as much as she can. This begins with getting the client to pay the ten percent agent's commission on top of your scale. This means you gross the scale amount and the agent gets her ten percent.

Contracts, in union commercials, are signed on the set. If you have any questions, call your agent before you sign. Keep your copy and get it to your agent.

Don't work without the contract, make sure it says principal if you are a principal. If you're booked as an extra, and don't do principal work without an upgraded contract. They don't get to book 3 extras, shoot tham as principals and upgrade only the one they like. It's best to call your agent and have her renegotiate your contract _before_ you begin shooting.

What do I do when I get to the set?

If you are booked you will be given a call time and a location. This may come from your agent or from a production assistant on the shoot. Waiting for a call time can be nerve wracking if you have other plans to consider but, like a watched pot never boiling, there is nothing you can do except stay near a phone or beeper.

Does it matter what I wear?

A wardrobe person will call you and tell you what you are expected to bring to the shoot. This is unless they have a specific costume for you. Generally you supply your own clothing. Good news- on union shoots you get paid. Fifteen dollars for each outfit you wear on camera- twenty five if it's evening clothes. Make sure that when you sign your contract the wardrobe fee is correct.

There will always be different requirements for clothing. The only constants are no stripes, really busy patterns or clothing with designer or manufacture logos. Each call will have color and season requirements. They will ask for lots of options. Pack them. Make sure everything is clean and pressed, hems are in and buttons are on. The joke is that after you've schlepped forty pounds of clothes across town, the wardrobe person will choose what you have on.

Wardrobe may also have clothes on the shoot for you. Good

news here too. More often than not you can buy these clothes at the end of the shoot for about half what the costumer paid for them. I've gotten some terrific "Mom In The Van" Gap outfits that way. It's not a bad idea to put such purchases directly and exclusively into your audition closet. If that's what they are going to put you in eventually why not help the audition process along by showing up like that?

Don't fight with the wardrobe person. There are reasons why they choose what they do. I don't know any who are trying to make you look bad- unless you're supposed to be the geek in the spot and if you don't know that, you need a different book than this and perhaps several years of therapy. This is not the prom. It's not up to you. What you wear is up to the costumer and the director.

What about my hair, or make-up?

On almost all union commercial shots there will be someone there to do hair and make-up for the principals. Come with a clean unmade-up face and clean hair. They'll do the rest. If you are an extra, you're on your own. More of that when discussing extras.

Where do I go when I get to the shoot location?

When you get to the set, check in. Someone, usually a production assistant (called a P.A.) will tell you where to put your stuff. He will alert the director and wardrobe that you have arrived. There is always lots of food. Constant food and lots of it. The table is replenished every thirty seconds. So have a cup of coffee, a bage,l and sit tight. They'll get to you. The standard operating procedure on any shoot is hurry up and wait.

Once you are in hair, make-up and wardrobe, be supremely careful of what you eat and drink and how you do it. Avoid anyone who might spill on you. You have to be telepathic.

Let the Assistant Director (the A.D.) or whoever is in charge of you, know where you are and then stay there. Rehearse if you need to or just keep yourself busy with a book, the paper, or your knitting. These, of course, you have brought with you. Try to stay quiet and centered and save your energy. Watch how much caffeine or sugar you ingest if you have a problem with it. Maintain a pleasant attitude toward everyone. Actors sometimes get a bad rap for being superior. Don't let that be you.

Keep in touch with your service or answering machine during the day. Keep your beeper with you but don't let it go off and spoil the shot. Find out where the pay phone is and have your change handy. Calling cards are great in an emergency but you can sometimes get stiffed with terrible bills depending on the phone you use.

Will we jump right in once they call for me?

When you are called to the set know that it is first for lighting. There is a lot of standing around while lights are set and camera angles fixed. Once all starts to go, you know what to do. Listen to the director, follow the instructions, roll with the punches and be wonderful. You may not understand why some things are done but then, in many cases, you don't have to.

If you break for lunch, remember the basic rule of "The crew eats first." They have to get back before you do. The food on shoots is usually very good but watch that you don't destroy your costume. Changing back into your own clothes is wise.

On most shoots, an hour for lunch is figured into your contract. Keep track of your time. Overtime can pay off very handsomely. Of course the longer the shoot takes, the more it will be costing the client, so be prepared for possible short tempers.

If you are shooting a commercial with a star, be respectful. In Chicago we get to do commercials with sports stars- I once played basketball with Michael Jordan. Let them come to you. Sometimes you will be requested not to talk to the star or ask for pictures or autographs. Be cool. Often the star is besieged by the client to meet and greet with him and whomever he is trying to impress. If you get to talk with a legend- great, if not, at least you were on the same shoot.

And when we're done?

Once the shoot, or your part of it, is finished and you have been released, put away whatever wardrobe is not yours, pack up your own belongings and sign out. Make sure your hours are correct on the sign-out sheet and that everything is set on your contract. Thank everyone, if they are not in the midst of another shot.

When you get home, call your agent and report back. Give her your hours and get her a copy of your contract. Then celebrate your good work and good fortune.

THEATRE

What kinds of theatre roles are available in Chicago?

About the only theatre in Chicago to which Chicago-based actors do not have access for employment are national tours originating from New York or elsewhere. There are often supplementary auditions held here so even that is not entirely closed to us. It is rare that a Chicago-based actor appears at the Shubert, Arie Crown, Chicago or Auditorium theatres, but once in a while it happens. Chicago actors have even done the translations for the plays which come here from around the world for the International Theatre Festival.

Are all theatre jobs union?

Unlike New York, you can actually do theatre, good theatre, which critics will come and see, without joining the union. This is important to remember. New York actors really do not understand this.

Theatre in Chicago is divided into Equity or non-Equity. In some cases, non-union members may act in Equity productions; however, union members may never (except in rare cases of waivers) appear in non-union productions. Those members who have scabbed have usually been caught and disciplined. It is not a good idea.

Theatre in Chicago is also divided between for profit and not-for-profit. A for-profit theatre or production simply means they are, in the eyes of the Internal Revenue Service, a commercial enterprise. They intend to make a profit. They raise money by selling shares in the production and hope the play runs forever so the investors make a ton of money.

A not-for-profit on the other hand has the same standing with the IRS as does a church or charity. Their *main* purpose is not to make money. They make art. Union affiliations are not dictated by for profit and not-for-profit status. You must investigate and know the company's union status before auditioning.

Which are the union for profit houses?

Apart from the aforementioned houses which bring in national tours and rarely hire actors here, examples of for-profit Equity theatres are the Marriott Lincolnshire, Drury Lane, Candlelight, the Forum, the Royal George, Briar Street. There are others.

These theatres hire union actors almost exclusively and pay very well- for Chicago theatre. The shows at Marriott and Drury Lane are almost exclusively musicals. The theatres are very large and fancy and the actors put in a long week which includes several matinee performances. If you are lucky enough to be a triple threat (actor, singer and dancer), becoming a regular with these theatres can afford you a busy, well-paid life.

Shear Madness has been running for years at the Mayfair Theatre. It is a an audience-interactive mystery spoof which has been wildly successful. Many Chicago actors have worked for them and a few have bought three flats as a result. It's great fun. It ain't Sophocles but it's every bit as tough. And if at least one of the points of theatre is to entertain, it truly does that.

Fox Theatricals runs to the latest non-musical Broadway hits, *Six Degrees Of Separation, Lost In Yonkers.* Perkins Productions also does New York hits such as *Angels In America.* These, once again, are for-profit union houses and pay well.

The union theatres which are not-for-profit, the Goodman, Steppenwolf, Victory Gardens, Court and many others, are the first generation of the now famous Chicago theatre explosion. Theirs are the histories of ground breaking productions, global press and first row ranking in the pantheon of Chicago theatres. Their seasons may be inconsistently successful but they are the perennials. The other well-known, union, not-for-profit theatres include Remains, National Jewish, Northlight and Wisdom Bridge. Shakespeare Repertory has been very successful presenting only two or three mainstage shows a year.

Alas, some Equity houses have fallen on hard times and are either on hiatus, being used as rental houses or have decided to produce on a non-Equity basis. But things change. Sometimes very rapidly. You will often find that is the rule in Chicago. Additionally, the demise of a theatre, such as the venerable Body Politic, has sometimes been announced prematurely. Old theatres die hard.

Then there are the many, many, non-union, not-for-profit theatre companies. New ones spring up every hour, it seems. Some stay a show or a season and then disband, some stay and grow. The majority do not pay at all, some a little. But almost all have a complimentary ticket offer for their actors, so at least your friends and family may see your work for free.

Another benefit, beyond resume credits, of non-union, not-for-profit theatre is many of them do get reviewed by the critics. Reviews are a great way to get noticed by the bigger theatres and directors because they all read them (even though they may claim not to).

Smaller not-for-profit theatres are located in dozens of neighborhoods, some of them not very nice. It is wise to investigate where you are going if you are unfamiliar with the company.

There is also community theatre, done in church basements and Park District field houses. This is fine and fun and, in all senses of the word, amateur. This does not get reviewed, even though some Park District shows may get invited to the Park District's jewel in the crown, Theatre on the Lake, in the summer, which sells out four hundred seats every performance. This is for the hobbyist. Here you "try out" and go to "play practice" instead of auditioning and rehearsing. You may, if you really want to be an actor, begin here. But if you aspire to ever quit your day job, you will move into the small off Loop theatre quickly. No one disdains community theatre but it is not considered professional or even pseudo-professional. It is the post-college equivalent of the Sophomore class play.

What, basically, are the differences between union and non-union theatre in Chicago?

The amount of money you get paid and how long or how often you have to work to get it.

This is the rule. There are, of course, exceptions. But generally in non-union theatre you will be paid nothing, beer money, very little to maybe a hundred bucks a week or so. But you are working and as I said earlier, being reviewed. You are getting a name for yourself and networking and those are both necessary here. Non-union work, good non-union work, is taken seriously.

Many people say that it is wise to spend a fair few years at this level. As explained elsewhere, you don't want to be in a rush to get your Equity card. Not without a good solid reputation and a formidable network.

You are, however, without a union to regulate rehearsal hours, theatre conditions and to secure a bond to insure that you will be paid. Rehearsals will be at night because everyone works during the day. They may last a long time and there may not be scheduled breaks. You may have to lend a hand building the set or getting the costumes. You may rehearse a long time because you can only rehearse a few hours at night.

You can be exploited and have no recourse. But, once again, you are working. And you can console yourself with the legends of Steppenwolf and how they all typed by day, rehearsed by night and scrubbed the toilets in the church basement before each show.

As for union houses: you have many rules, many perks and less work. You will be paid according to the contract which the theatre has signed with Equity. Chicago union houses work, generally, under either the LORT (League of Regional Theatres) or CAT (Chicago Area Theatres) contract. There are several tiers for each contract. The tiers are decided by the profit status and the size of each house.

This determines the paycheck and the number of performances.

Also covered by the union are showcases, readings and Theatre for Young Audience(TYA) as well as other special "occasional" contracts. Equity members may choose to put up a production on their own, a showcase. They are not paid and the union regulates the number of performances. They may use a non-union house. This is growing both in popularity and respect. Equity members can participate in staged readings. They are paid a stipend for the readings and the rehearsal. Both the hours of rehearsal and the number of performances are limited by the union. Children's theatre is produced often under the Theatre For Young Audiences contract. The pay isn't anything to retire to the South of France on, but it does pay.

There are also informal readings of new plays. Theatres and playwrights do this from time to time. These are very casual and for this you are neither rehearsed or paid. You might get a beer. You will get heard and meet new folks.

On occasion, an Equity member can be used in a non Equity production when an Equity waiver has been approved. This is not common but does happen.

Working in an Equity show, you will rehearse for a set number of hours each day for two to three weeks. Regular breaks are scheduled. Overtime will cost the producer. The space must be clean and safe. There must be a cot. Actors don't build the set. Lots of rules.

You are paid for rehearsal. You are paid for understudying. A portion of your salary goes into your pension and welfare. There is insurance offered, if you earn enough you can qualify. If you work a certain number of weeks, you get paid vacation money. Most importantly YOU GET PAID. And, if for some reason the checks are late or rubber, you have recourse. The union will take care of it.

For this you pay union dues and abide by the union rules. This is not hard to follow. The perks are you get to play with the big kids and be pretty much treated like a big kid. The draw back, if you choose to see it as that, is that you can't, willy-nilly, go back and play with the other guys.

As mentioned elsewhere, Equity houses doing large shows and with tight budgets will occasionally hire non-union actors once the Equity quota is met. This is a great opportunity for non-union actors to see just how green the grass is, to do a good job and be noticed and to network.

Why, if you are Equity, would you want to do a showcase, i.e., work for free?

It's all in the verb- WORK. There is not enough good Equity work to go around. Heck, there just isn't enough Equity work period. So it may well be that a group of like-minded souls decide to produce themselves. A lot of work. More than anyone imagined but also a chance to hustle the agents, casting directors and artistic directors in to see you doing something in which you plan to shine.

Showcases are becoming very popular. They are not regarded as the last resort of the hard core unemployables. Good working actors will work for free if they believe in the piece. Actors who have a relationship with "the powers that be" can get those decision-making bodies into the seats and thereby benefit the rest of the cast.

How do I get hired?

Ninety-nine times out of a hundred, you audition. The odd time you will just be offered a role by a director who knows you. But for the most part you audition.

There are also general auditions. Theatres hold these annually, mainly during the summer months. For generals, actors are asked to prepare one or two monologues which show them off. You bring a picture and resume (bring several). It's a good way for a theatre to get to know you if you are new. Some established actors will go anyway and present a piece which shows them in a new light.

Anywhere from two to twenty or more theatre companies may participate. This is a chance to put you through the agony of auditioning only once. You prepare your pieces and bring tons of pictures and resumes. A good use of everyone's time.

Theatres will then call actors in, sometimes as a result of generals, to audition for specific roles in upcoming productions. For this you are asked to prepare either a piece from the specific play (your choice of material or assigned sides) or a monologue of your choosing.

It is wise to prepare all along for auditions in which a prepared piece is required. Keep yourself busy finding monologues you perform well, really like, and whow who you are. An audition piece, I feel, is a job interview using someone else's words.

Have plenty of monologues to choose from so that you can tailor your audition to the theatre's requirements without having to scurry over hell's half acre to find a piece and cram it into your soul in twenty-four hours.

It may also happen that once you've performed your two pieces, you may be asked if you have anything else. Then you can flash your pack and bowl them over with your range, repertoire and professionalism. Boy Scouts and actors must always be prepared.

The theatre will let you know ahead of time what sort of material to prepare and how long it should be. DO WHAT THEY ASK. It is not worth it to break the rules here. Prepare your monologues to fit their requirements. If they ask for classical, don't try to sneak by a little Mamet. If they ask for works from their season, put in the effort and prepare those. If they are open to whatever you choose, then do your homework and find out what the season is, what kinds of plays they usually do and those they just did. Unless you knock the socks off their Hamlet, I'd forget "To be or not..." if the theatre did Hamlet in the last few years. Be smart.

Is it better to be outrageous and different in a monologue,

or just straight?

Whatever shows YOU off best. Your skills, strengths and range.

If they ask for a dialect, do it. If you do it well, great. If you are rocky, get a coach. Otherwise do not do monologues in dialect for a general audition. Have some prepared in case they ask for them but don't make a dialect piece your only offering.

Auditors are very tired of abusive language, obscenity, screaming and recounting your first sexual encounter. You don't have to scream to be dramatic. Comedy doesn't mean stand-up, or fall down. Gay-bashing, men-bashing, women-bashing... can't we find anything else? You try sitting in a room all day having fifty actors one after another come in and talk about their or other's private parts and what they or someone else have or can do with them. Palls some.

And have someone- other than your mother unless she is Uta Hagen- work with you on your audition. A friend you trust or a coach you trust is worth the money. You need another pair of ears and eyes.

And for heaven's sake, time your pieces and make absolutely sure that they are not over the time limit. Shorter is better. Directors usually know all they need to in the first fifteen seconds of your monologue. That's not because you are bad at it; it's because they are good. A minute to a minute and a half is swell.

Directors really hate it if the pieces run overtime. It says many things: the actor is careless or arrogant, he thinks the rules apply to everyone else or he can't follow directions. Now aren't you just dying to cast this guy?

Additionally, overtime pieces screw up the schedule and then everyone else is inconvenienced. If a director is getting antsy about time and is looking at his watch, guess what, he's not watching your brilliant performance. And boy, is it fun to be cut off and told thank you just as the monologue crescendos. Just time them. Cut them. But bring them in under the time limit. There's truth in the adage of leaving them wanting more.

If you are asked to prepare a scene or monologue from the play, do so. Be prepared. Show yourself at your very best advantage. This may mean asking a coach to look at your audition scene or monologue.

Prepare. Read the whole play, not just the sides. The theatre should make the play available for actors to read it there. Act One Bookstore will sometimes have a reading copy. Better yet, buy the script if you can. Inspiration doesn't always hit during business hours.

You may be asked to a call back, or a second call back. You may be asked to read with different people. Don't go suicidal if you don't get the part. Drop them a note wishing them luck and thanking them. You'll get another chance.

What do I do when I get to the audition?

If you are an Equity member or an Equity Membership Candidate, you must show your up-to-date Equity card to the monitor. Don't forget your card. It is not pleasant if you do.

Always bring plenty of pictures and resumes - more than you'll need. Make sure they are clean, crisp and up-to-date. Of course you can write in a VERY recent addition such as a role in which you are currently appearing, but really they should always be up to date.

Unlike commercial and film auditions, you can and should put your home telephone number on the resume. That is, unless you are being submitted by an agent. Include all your phone numbers, service, beeper etc.

You'll be asked to fill in a registration form. These vary widely. Just fill it in and don't try to be funny. Save the yuks for your comic piece. Be absolutely truthful. If they ask if you sing and you don't, do everyone a favor and tell the truth. Ditto dancing, juggling and stage combat. They are going to find out, why get off on the wrong foot and be known as a liar?

When I do get an audition, other than being prepared, what do I do?

Just what you do in any other audition. Show up on time. Don't be too early. Sign in. Be polite to the monitor. Be quiet in the lobby. Don't waste your energy chatting. Don't invade other actors' privacy. Be ready. Be pleasant but business-like when you go in. Some directors do not like to shake hands so don't extend yours until his is offered to you.

Chat if they want to chat. When they ask you what you will be doing, say the names of the pieces and the character. All you need to say is "I'm doing Jeff from *Walk, Trot Canter* and Hamlet." You don't have to give playwrights' names and you really shouldn't explain the piece. They don't need to know that you just shot your mother or won the Nobel Prize or both. If you are doing one of the biggies from Shakespeare or the Greeks, you don't need to say the play. I mean really, how many Macbeths are there?

Never address your monologue directly to the auditors. They don't like this because it forces them to interact with you instead of allowing them to watch. Set your focus in the middle distance, above their heads or just off to the sides.

You may use a chair if there is one. But ask first. Never disturb the set of whatever show the theatre is running at the time of the audition. For God's sake don't throw anything. Don't bring props.

If you are auditioning for a specific role in a specific play and have prepared a scene, listen to what the director asks you to do with it, then do that to the best of your powers. If you have not been paired with another actor out in the hallway or lobby, you will be given a reader with whom to read once you enter the audition. Be nice to him.

If you mess up on your lines, don't swear. Just ask to begin again. If you think you did not do well, don't apologize. You may very well have fooled them.

The director may ask you to do the scene again. Listen to the directions and follow them. Make the adjustments. Let him see that you cannot only listen to and digest directions but also that you are wonderfully versatile.

When you are finished, say thank you and leave. Don't dawdle and chatter. The director may be thinking how wonderful you were. Don't pop the bubble.

What do I wear to an audition?

Unless you are auditioning for a specific role, wear clean, neat, comfortable clothes. Don't hide under layers of big sweaters. They may wonder if you look like John Merrick. Sexy, obviously unsubtle, clothes are dangerous. I wouldn't.

Make yourself look good, pleasant and sane. Dress like the person you would like to cast if your name, your career, the futures of your children and a whole lot of other people's money were hanging in the balance. Be clean. And, for God's sake, not hung over.

What if I am trying to look right for a specific role?

Then dress for it. I take the advice that a suggestion is much better than a full blown costume, but that is only one opinion. Of course you're not going to dress like Madonna to play Saint Joan- unless, God help you, that's the director's concept. In that case you may want to rethink auditioning at all.

It's fun to alter your appearance a bit for auditions. I do, however, think going all-out looks a bit desperate- overeager. Ladies should wear a longish skirt to read for Shakespeare, but me, I'd leave the wimple at home.

How do you find out about an audition?

For theatre, very rarely through your agent. Sometimes union, for-profit, and some not-for-profit theatres will take submissions for auditions, but that's not the norm in Chicago. However, if you hear of something you very much want to do, you should call your agent and ask to be read.

If a theatre knows you, they will call you to ask you to read. That's where all that famous networking and showcasing and shameless self-promotion comes into play. Someone from the theatre will call and ask if you are interested and then will schedule you a time.

You may hear through word-of-mouth. Not the most reliable. Find somewhere to check it out. That's a good job for your agent on a slow Tuesday.

Most actors find out about jobs through the Equity or Non-Equity telephone hotlines or through the listings in PerformInk, the actors' trade paper. There are other publications which have some listings, like Audition News and the Reader, but those in the know use the hotlines and PerformInk.

It will come as no surprise that there are far more auditions printed in these publications for non-union (also referred to as non-eligible) than there are for Equity work. Equity actors rely almost exclusively on direct calls from the theatre or the Equity hotline. The hotline is a tape with listings of auditions, actors' nights and other upcoming Equity business such as meetings or elections.

You will be told what theatre is casting and for what show or shows. Generals are also announced. The same holds for the non-Equity line. The information appears, obviously, in printed form in PerformInk which is published every other Thursday.

Once I know about an audition, how do I get in?

Presuming no one called you and asked you and that the auditions are open, you would call the number at the appropriate time and make an appointment. That translates to: the listing (either taped or written) will give the dates of the audition, the location, the number to call to schedule an audition time and the date and time someone will be at the number to make that appointment.

For Equity auditions you most often are instructed to call the

Equity appointments number between certain hours on a given day. Needless to say, if this is a hot audition the lines will be lighting up one second past ten a.m. So put the telephone next to the coffee pot and keep your finger poised over the redial button. Sometimes you are instructed to phone the theatre. This is the more usual procedure in scheduling non-Equity auditions.

How do I know these auditions are real and that the theatres are on the up-and-up?

A healthy dose of cynicism will do you well in this business. In the case of Equity theatres, you know they are on the up-and-up because they have had to post a bond and sign various agreements with the Union. As for non-union, if it is a well-known, well established theatre, you can bet they are on the up-and-up. Otherwise you take your chances.

What do I do after an audition?

After you have done your audition, thank them and leave. Don't dash for the door as if the theatre were on fire, but don't linger looking pathetic. Thank the stage manager, audition assistant or monitor on the way out. Take a moment to think about what you did. Dig for any ray of hope in the words the director gave you. Write the director a note wishing him luck with the production.

Then forget the audition. Be delightfully surprised if they call you back, but otherwise let it go. You are going to get what you are going to get. I used to hang on till the bitter end hoping to be cast, I'd believe that there was still a chance until I got to the theatre on opening night, opened the program and my name wasn't there. This is not healthy. Let it go and concentrate on the next project.

What are Actors' Nights?

Actors and other show biz folks get in free! Theatres, when a show is not selling well, or sometimes out of the goodness of their hearts, will announce an actors' night. Equity actors' nights require that you make a reservation and that you present your Equity card when you collect the tickets. You are generally allowed two tickets per Equity card. Non-union houses will often ask you to bring a headshot and resume as proof that you are mad enough to be in this business.

Actors' nights are a great free way to see plays. You can also schmooze in the lobby. It's a good way to see what the theatres are doing and decide which theatres you would want to work for.

What about play readings?

Many theatres will have play readings on off nights. Others, like the Chicago Dramatists Workshop, are solely dedicated to such presentations. To be asked to read is great. It's a nice showcase and network opportunity. Attending them is also a good idea. You get to see new works and generally get into the loop.

There are, of course, some weirdos who go to these for the discussions afterwards. I think they are not allowed to speak at home and attend readings to inflict their asinine opinions on a captive audience too polite to tell them to shut up. They don't always show up, take comfort. And this is about the only downside to readings.

What is a workshop?

Sometimes a script is not quite ready for production and a theatre will get a grant or somehow find the money to workshop it. This means that it is cast and the cast, director and playwright wrestle with it for some weeks. It's a wonderful process and you can learn a great deal about many, many aspects of theatre.

Should I agree to be an understudy if I'm asked?

You will often be asked at an audition whether you are willing, if not cast, to understudy. Consider your decision. The conditions of employment vary from theatre to theatre. You may or may not be paid if you are non-Equity or working in a non-Equity house. Many Equity houses hire non-Equity understudies and do pay. You may, having been cast, be asked to understudy another (often larger) role and for this you will often receive extra pay.

Before accepting any job you should be very sure about rehearsals, compensation, and the chance of going on. The first two are more easily spelled out, the third a matter of chance, although in some cases the theatre may know of an actor's conflicts in advance. Be absolutely sure you understand all the information and responsibilities before accepting the job.

THEN LEARN THE LINES. I cannot stress this strongly enough. Ask any director, any stage manager and they will say the same thing, often in more colorful language. Even before the rehearsals start, before those 'real' actors have theirs down, LEARN THE LINES. "You know not the day nor the hour." Spend your energy learning the lines, not making excuses as to why you couldn't. As an understudy you don't have the luxury of rehearsal before opening in which to pound in the words. Use a tape recorder. Abuse your friends. Do whatever is necessary, but learn them. Think how smug you will feel when that actor you are understudying is searching for the words that are now etched in your memory. Warning: however smug you may feel, resist the temptation to prompt. That's not your job.

Another refrain heard from directors and stage managers is: TAKE IT SERIOUSLY. You're not "just the understudy." You were asked to take on the responsibility because they thought you could do something very difficult. Prove it to them. Attend all the rehearsals you possibly can. Take notes. Record the blocking. If you miss it in rehearsal, check with the stage manager. If you miss rehearsals, check with the stage manager.

Be ready at any moment to step into the role. Even if the actor is out for a few minutes, you can make an excellent impression by being able to seemlessly blend in to the rehearsal. Might also keep the other actor on his toes. TAKE THE INITIATIVE. Just as you made it a point to get to rehearsals, get to performances regularly, because plays change after opening, whatever the director may say. The Stage Manager will always be able to get you a seat.

When rehearsing and especially if you do have to go on, maintain the integrity and intentions of the production as directed and of the role as it has been directed and is being played. This is not the time to play it as it *should* be played, to show them all what they missed. Save that for your own production. Do not initiate physical or vocal changes. Your job is to reproduce, as best as possible, the performance of the actor you have been understudying. The temptation to change or embellish is great, but resist it.

If you have done your job and do not let the nerves take over, you will be fine. The Stage Manager will thank you forever. If you are unprepared, that will be remembered perpetually as well. If you do get to go on, you can put the role on your resume. And if you don't? If you have done all the work, been prepared and the final curtain comes down and you're still on the wrong side of the footlights, what then? You can use the credit, indicating understudy, on your resume. You have learned a great deal by watching. You have disciplined yourself. Whatever you have done, good or bad, has been noted and will be remembered by Stage Managers, directors, staff and actors. I can think of any number of actors who proved themselves serious and responsible by their professional performances that were never seen by audiences. They are hired again and again in ever more important capacities. The effort, commitment and sometimes monumental frustration are really worth it, but only if you TAKE IT SERIOUSLY.

What do I need to know when I am cast in a play?

Other than your lines and blocking? Aside from the usual admonitions to be on time and sober, to treat everyone well, to hang up your clothes etc., I would add that being in a production is a great way to be seen by casting folks but they must be told you're there. So, send them a flyer with a note, or have postcards made of your headshot and send them around. The only person you can pester by phone is your agent. And if your agent can't be bothered to get to see your show over the four or more week run, you might consider getting a new agent. Some Chicago agents, directors and casting people are very good about getting to theatre. Others... You should be able to get free tickets for these professionals from the theatre.

If you know that a director, casting type, etc., has come to see your show, you can, of course, write to them afterwards saying that you hope they enjoyed the play and here is your picture and resume.

Some things they might not have taught you in drama school but which you need to know.... Never be late. If you think that you might just possibly be late, phone the stage manager.

Never give another actor notes- unless they specifically ask. If you have a gripe about another actor's behavior or performance during a run, go to the stage manager. The director is rarely there. Work through the stage manager rather than directly confronting the other actor.

Never touch anything on the prop table that isn't yours but always check your props before the show. Don't change a prop or add one or decide not to use it without clearing all this with the director and stage manager.

Take care of your costume. Hang it up. Don't eat or drink white you're wearing it. If something is ripped or broken, tell the wardrobe people at the earliest convenient moment. Don't wait until five minutes before your entrance. Never take your costume home. Don't add or subtract from your costume. That applies to make-up as well. If you are given something new to wear or carry, make sure that everyone with whom you deal on stage has been introduced to the new item before you go on. It's very disconcerting to meet a new wig for the first time on stage in front of a full house.

Never alter your performance without checking and receiving permission from the director. Any changes need to be rehearsed.

This includes saying all the lines as they are written- not your improvements.

Never cut, color or in anyway change your hair during a rehearsal or run without consulting the stage manager. This applies to facial hair as well.

Never goof around on stage. You will crack up some fellow performers but you will annoy and alienate a great many more. Practical jokes aren't one bit funny. Outrageous ad libs are out as well.

Pay attention and make all your entrances. Save your performance for the stage, not the green room. Don't come in exhausted or hung over. Part of your job is staying well and well rested.

Don't quit one show to go into another without giving adequate notice.

Respect your fellow cast members' needs for preparation. Don't talk before a show if they need to be quiet.

Keep your dressing room space neat and clean. Some Chicago theatres are tiny and the dressing rooms cramped. You can make the best of a bad situation by being tidy and considerate.

Be kind and considerate to everyone involved in the production. Actors can make themselves very unpopular if for some ridiculous reason they think themselves better than the rest of the theatre team.

If you are asked to pitch in and help, do so. Don't be above it.

Get your picture and your "bio" for the program into the stage manager when asked. And write a real bio. Phony ones scream phony. Resist the temptation to be too cute.

Read your script every day during a run.

If things get stale or you begin to loose a laugh, go back to basics. Listen, as if for the first time. Let yourself be surprised.

Never hate the audience.

Never push a moment, a line, a fellow actor or the audience. Only push yourself to be your very best. Sometimes that means being very small. But if that's the size you are meant to be, be it.

Anything else?

Yes, enjoy! Celebrate. Ours is a rare and wonderful gift. Granted it's tough and we eat a lot of macaroni and cheese, but we should love it. If you ever feel tired backstage and think maybe you'll just phone it in tonight, think of all the nights you'll be alone in your living room and wishing to have this chance back. Enjoy every single moment. Learn and grow.

And when it's time to get out, for a little while or for good, be able to do so. There is no shame. Things pass. Times change. You need different things at different stages of your life. If this no longer gives you joy, find something that does. Misery reads across the proverbial footlights. Find something else and don't be ashamed to leave.

But until that time- perhaps it never will come to you- relish every moment. Be open and alive and know that you are part of a very ancient family. In the beginning they told stories. Around a cave fire they told of the hunt and the bravery of the tribe. It's grown a bit more sophisticated over the millennia, but that is in effect what we do every Friday night at eight. We tell the story.

VOICE-OVER

What is a voice-over?

A voice-over is a radio commercial or the voice-only part of a television commercial. Additionally, voice-over is used in industrials, generally as a narrator. Or as an unseen voice narrating a film or television program.

What is NOT voice-over?

It is not radio drama, radio newscasting, chat show host or disc jockey. Books on tape don't technically qualify as voice-over.

Do I need to belong to a union?

Yes, if you want to make good money and be protected. Whereas some ad agencies, even the larger ones, are experimenting with using non-union talent in an effort to save money, the vast majority of the big time voice-over work is union. There are both SAG and AFTRA voice-overs. Once again, be aware of your union status.

As I said earlier, some ad agencies in this rough economy are experimenting with non-union work so that they do not have to pay scale or residuals. They do what is called a buy-out. You are paid for your session fee and that's the end of it. The agencies are complaining however that they cannot get the same quality of talent using non-union newcomers. Voice-over is a demanding business and, as with everything else, you get what you pay for.

Can I make a living in voice-overs?

If you're very lucky and very good you can. There are some actors who make quite a handsome living doing nothing but voice-over. They are well established, work at self-promotion ceaselessly and always deliver. They do the lion share of the work. And they are almost always men.

Inequitable as it may seem, something in the neighborhood of eighty percent of the voice-over work in Chicago has gone to men. A small percentage of that eighty percent gets the greatest percent of the work.

What do I need?

You need an excellent demo tape, a hard working agent, a hide of iron, a great voice and an ability to read copy in a clear, engaging, lively manner in under thirty seconds.

First, the tape. You cannot get your foot in the door without a tape. You will spend a great deal of money to produce a good one but any money spent producing anything less than top quality is money thrown down the drain. You never get a second chance to make a first impression and the talent buyer will hear your tape long before she sees you- if at all.

Before you sink a good chunk of your hard earned money into a voice tape, decide if this is what you really want. Know that the competition is very stiff. Listen to an expert, not your mother or her hairdresser, to know if you have what it takes. Ask your agent, and hope you've got a real agent- one who knows and will take the time to guide your career.

Where do I get a tape made?

There are a number of places where you can go to get a demo tape produced in Chicago. Beware of voice tape factories where they pull the same dog-eared copy out of the file drawer for everyone. You need to spend a good long time talking with your producer, tailoring material that is just right for you. Some producers, the good ones, will write the copy just for you. If your agent can't recommend a producer or studio, ask around. Screen Magazine's annual *Chicago Production Bible* also lists all the producers, studios and tape duplication services.

Make sure your producer goes into the studio with you and that you go to a first class studio- not your Uncle Erwin's basement. A cheap tape is the equivelant of a 4-for-a-dollar headshot.

Your producer should direct you and then work with the engineer to cut the tape perfectly after they have added music and sound. The tape should run no more than two and a half minutes and highlight your special quality. It should show a variety of what you can do. Sometimes dialogue with another actor (one who knows what he or she is doing) is a plus. Whereas dialects are nice, there isn't a big market for them.

You are looking at something in the neighborhood of two thousand dollars for five hundred copies. And yes, you will need that many. And you haven't even started on the artwork yet. What art work? You need a J-card.

A J-card is the piece of cardstock paper that is folded in a somewhat 'J' like configuration and slips into your plastic tape box. They're the front pieces in cassette tapes you buy that have the band's name on the front and the songs and liner notes on the inside. Got it?

You need a good graphic artist for your J-card. You need snappy graphics that tell people who you are, that catch the eye and jog the memory. There are thousands of tapes out there. Yours needs to stand out. Some people put their picture on their J-cards. Others argue that if the client doesn't think, looking at your picture, that you look like the sound he wants, it doesn't matter what you sound like. Go figure. But get a really first class J-card. You may also want to get postcards with the same logo on them. These are for the wave after wave of self-promotion in which you must engage.

Your J-card needs your name and agent on it and a contact number. A list of the spots and maybe the producer's and engineer's names is also good. The tape itself should have a sticker on it with your name, your agent and a contact number. Why? Because little tapes sometimes stray from their boxes. Use your agent's telephone number, not your own. If you are multi-listed for voice-over work, make sure that you have tapes with each agent's name on them. Or you may choose to mark the tape with "agencies" meaning that the talent buyer can call his favorite agency to find you. Some actors use an answering service number. Whatever you and your agent decide on, make sure that there is a good, reliable contact number on the tape.

A good producer should be able to direct you through all this as well as the distribution.

How do I get the tapes in the hands of voice-over talent buyers?

Oh, the world of distribution! Don't count on your agent to distribute your tapes. They need to be given a dozen or so- or however many they ask for- but you do the bulk of the distribution. Your agent will give you a list of people to whom you should send the tape. This list is comprised primarily of creatives from ad agencies. Make sure the list is up to the second because the turn-over in ad agencies can be sudden and massive. Producers will also be on the list. Check these names and addresses as well. Create a brief cover letter to accompany your tape. Work with your agent on this. Then start stuffing and schlepping.

Some tapes you will mail. These go to out-of-the-way agencies and producers. You will discover that the fastest, cheapest and surest way to get the majority of your tapes distributed is to deliver them yourself. Hand address or use printed labels from your agent, package them and then bag them by agency. Don't try to carry more than you can handle. Find the agencies that are in the same neighborhood (and many are) and make a run.

Your destination is the mail room and, with your most winning smile, ask the nice people in the mail room to please see that these tapes get into the right hands. The mail room employees are aware of the time and money you put into this enterprise and will often sort through the tapes to make sure that the people to whom you addressed them are, in fact, still with the agency. Thank them and then go off with the next load.

After that? Here, there is much discussion. Some actors say

you should attempt to get to the creatives and play your tape for them. Some say that creatives look upon meeting with a voice-over actor with the same loathing they face oral surgery.

There are a lot of really bad, half-baked, shoddily produced tapes vying for ear-time. Creatives who have listened to these inferior products, either voluntarily or because they were brow beaten by a pushy actor, sometimes get fed up. It is soul-destroying to think that those tapes into which your poured your heart, soul and a large chunk of cash will sit and gather dust on some copywriter's desk or be tossed out unheard. That's one of the toughest aspects of voice-over. You will have to devise a plan of action with your agent.

Always carry your voice-tapes with you- just as you do your headshot and resume. Take them to auditions. Check with your agents to make sure they have plenty on hand.

Some voice-over actors use gimmicks or presents. They will hand out pens with their names, highlighters, food. This is a cutthroat, fiercely competitive business and it takes a great deal to be noticed and remembered. We who work in voice-over joke about shameless self-promotion but it's a reality. Voice-over is a big deal. It takes a lot of time and effort, money and keeping your nose to the grindstone.

You need to keep up on which advertising people are at what agencies and handling which accounts. You need to practice. You need to know what voices are being used. You need to know the kinds of delivery for which you may be asked. You need to learn to sound like other voices. You have to be good at what you do. You also have to be good at being good and good at letting people know you are.

What do I do at a voice-over audition?

Well, you don't have to dress the part.

You will be called by your agent to come into her office or to go to an ad agency or recording studio. You'll sign in and be given the copy and any directions. Read over the copy. Know what the product is and how they want you to deliver the copy. Ask the pronunciation of any words with which you are unfamiliar. Know how long the spot is and work on getting your read to match the time.

Many actors will be careful of what they eat and drink before a voice-over audition or booking. Many will stay away from dairy products because they cause mucus which coats your pipes or makes you sound stuffed up or fuzzy. It's a truly stupid idea to stay out late in a loud and smoky bar or scream yourself hoarse at a ballgame the night before an audition. Unless, of course, they want you to sound like Harvey Fierstein.

Many actors, too, will warm up before an audition to get their teeth, lips, gums and faces moving. This is especially good if the copy is tricky or dense. If you are asked for a voice or a dialect, it's an excellent idea to prepare it some time earlier than two seconds before you face the microphone.

In the audition you will be asked to say the first line or so in order for the engineer to get a sound level. Then you will be asked to read the copy. You may get direction. Follow it. Ask questions if you are unsure of the director's wishes. Don't argue. Don't suggest changes in the text. Be pleasant. Be professional. Thank them and then leave.

You got it or you didn't. Recall what you did wrong or right. Act on both. Move on.

What do I do if I get the job?

Right after jumping up and down a lot? Once again, make sure your voice is in shape and warmed up and that any other homework is done. Make sure that you show up at the right studio at the right time. Be very familiar with the copy.

You'll meet and greet and go into the studio with the other actors who are recording- or you may be doing this on your own. Here comes the tricky part. The client may well be there. The client is the person who is paying for the whole shooting match and therefore gets to say whatever she likes as often as she likes. On the best of all possible sessions, she will be pleasant, articulate and know exactly what she wants. This will, in fact, be humanly possible to produce.

Then there are the other times. The sessions from hell. Nobody knows what they want, except that it isn't what the other client (known as "the suit") wants, what the ad agency creative told you or anything that has come out of your mouth since the session started. There are some suits who cannot understand that those words are unpronounceable as written or that you cannot possible say that many pages of copy in fifty seconds. You may get directions like this I heard first-hand: "Do it just like John Cleese, but younger, female and not English."

One voice-over veteran says that he looks on the other side of the glass in a recording studio, counts the number of suits and multiplies by fifteen minutes. That's how much longer than usual the process will take that day.

Have I scared you off? This is the exception, not the rule. The vast majority of voice-over sessions are very easy and pleasant. But it is well to be warned that things can get very hairy. You start to panic if you think it's just you and that this has never happened before in the history of recorded sound. Panic is your enemy in voice-over as in any aspect of this business. It wrecks your concentration and confidence and plays merry hell with your ego and performance. Know that stupid things can happen and that mistakes can be made. Sometimes, you will make them. Sometimes the other guy. Examine honestly what is going on and deal with it.

At the end of the session, perfect or otherwise, thank everyone and sign all the necessary paper work. Keep you copy of the contract and deliver it to your agent. Report your hours to her. Write a note to everyone involved saying that you enjoyed the experience and are looking forward to working with them again soon. Then wait to hear your round, pear-shaped tones over the airwaves.

How often do I make a new tape?

Tricky question. Ask your agent. A tape is good for a couple of years. As you get work, ask for copies of the spot and hold on to them. When you go to make a new tape you can use your already recorded work. That cuts down on the expense.

Do I need just one tape?

Boy, I wish I could say yes. But no. You need a commercial tape and a narration tape. A narration tape is for industrials, educational films and the like. Some of the really big boys have several tapes, ones with character voices, impersonations, dialogues. You need not get into that, just starting out. The basics are a commercial tape and a narration tape.

Remember, your tape is your first introduction. Your audition, your job interview. You have no picture and resume in this business. The tape is everything. The work has to be exceptional and the packaging memorable. They work together. You cannot get by without both.

Good luck.

INDUSTRIAL

Just exactly what is an industrial?

An industrial is a film made to teach or demonstrate. They can be highly technical- a film instructing employees in the inner workings of the new J472-A Knutsen valve, or psychological- illustrating the early signs of teenage depression and how to deal with them.

Industrials call for both spokespersons and day players. A spokesperson narrates the story or explains and guides the viewer through technical information. A day player is an actor being another person, the one with the problem or the one trying to solve it.

Some industrials are straightforward presentations of information. These are the "Here you see the way that by using the new withholding option 10-72, your client can save ..." type. Often the material to be covered is very complex and confusing. The narrator needs a clean delivery. In these cases, because of the highly technical language, the actor will use an ear prompter.

Other industrials are more dramatic. These will call for actors to play the role of people dealing with a new product or with a personal problem. A different kind of acting is demanded here. This is more like film acting in that you are telling a human story.

The variety of industrials is as wide as the variety of subjects about which they are made. Chicago is a very good market for industrials and there are actors who have carved a niche for themselves and earn a good living concentrating in this market. It can become your bread and butter. Several classes are taught throughout the city to train actors for this market.

Do I need to be a union member?

Both union and non-union industrials are shot in Chicago. If there is a question of union status, either yours or the producer's, be sure to clear it with your agent. As with any other work, you must be clear as to your union status and not attempt to work outside your status. No one involved is happy if an actor makes a mess of casting by being unclear or dishonest about his union standing.

Some industrials, as I said, are shot non-union. Union industrials can be under the jurisdiction of either SAG or AFTRA. Be sure you know before the audition which union is in charge. When you get to the audition, check again. Your agent may not have had the correct information. This is very important if you are not a fully-paid-up member of the union. Casting directors will have to clear you with the union and should they find a hitch which causes a problem they will be none too anxious to call you in again. If you are a fully-paid-up member of both unions and are in good standing, you have nothing to worry about- except getting the job.

An industrial audition is like any other. It will be held in your agent's office, in a casting office or at the client's or director's place of business. Come dressed appropriately for the role. There may be changes or you may be asked to read a different role, but prepare for the role for which you were initially called. You don't have to wear surgical scrubs when called for a doctor, but don't show up in jeans or straight from the gym either. This must, as with everything else, be business-like.

Your agent may be able to get you copy ahead of the audition. If so, learn it. If you are doing straight narration or a very long, technically involved explanation, you may want to put it on your ear prompter. Many, many casting directors have told me that they do not want actors who are reading for dramatic roles or have short narrations to use the ear. They say it is impossible to direct an actor who has already recorded his performance. Ear prompters can become both a crutch and an impediment.

On the other hand, (and acting in Chicago, as anywhere else, is full of contradictions) an ear prompter is almost a necessity if you are to be taken seriously as an industrial performer. Whether you use it extensively or not, it is very wise to be ear prompter proficient and to indicate this on your resume. Your agent may even insist on it. Agents make reels of their actors performing in simulated industrials and then send these reels out to potential industrial clients. They would like to be able to say that all the talent represented is ear prompter proficient.

Are there classes to learn how to use an ear prompter?

Ask your agent or agents. As with anything, never assume. Your agent may recommend a training center to learn to use the ear. There are a couple in Chicago. The instructors there will show you how the aid works and no doubt tell you where to get a good one. Make sure you practice.

And make sure you ask in the audition and at the shoot if you may use it. Many Chicago casting directors tell me that some clients don't want actors, particularly in dramatic scenes, to use the ear. Other clients, conversely, will demand that the spokesperson use the ear. You've got to be ready, informed and flexible. That rule applies to just about all phases of acting in Chicago- or anywhere.

As with a commercial audition, listen to and follow all directions. Do your very best job and then try to forget it. It's out of your hands and should go out of your mind, clearing space for the next audition. Don't fret. You are either going to get it or you are not and getting it depends on a myriad of factors beyond your acting ability. Learn and move forward.

CHILDREN

How do children go about getting acting work in Chicago?

I would first determine who it is who wants the child in this business. Okay, if the darling is a matter of weeks old, we can assume that it is the parents. This holds true into toddlerhood. Few children's first full sentences are "Get my agent on the phone and see if I'm still iced on that Sears job."

If a child is of an age when he can reasonably understand what is expected (and still wants to go ahead), then maybe the decision to give this a try can be his.

I say this because the business is chock-a-block with small fry whose parents have decided that they will be the next MacCauley Caulkin, Mason Gamble or Anna Chlumsky and come hell or high water, whether the little tyke likes it or no, he will be.

The money they make may pay for college if there's enough left over after the shrink gets through.

I have seen children wound up, dressed up and set up. In most cases the children start out fine, it's the parents who should be reprogrammed. Are you doing this because you never had a chance? Are you doing this so that you and the old man don't have to work? Are you doing this even though little Sydney cries or is constipated every time you trot him out? Maybe you ought to give Little League another think.

On the other hand there are some wonderful families in the business here in Chicago, whole families with their heads screwed on correctly and who realize this is a hobby for the kids, not the rent check or their entire psyches.

This business is grueling. The rejection is monumental. The stress, repetition and uncertainties can be crippling. Some of the people involved should not be allowed around other adults let alone small, impressionable children. Are you sure your child is up to this? On the other hand, the self-esteem some children gain is enormous and the financial rewards are not inconsiderable.

Well, that's pretty scary. How do I know if my child should be an actor?

If the child is a baby and you take him on an audition and he hates it and cries and clings to you, you've got a pretty clear indication. Stick with the Swim N' Gym at the YMCA. However, if the baby seems comfortable with all these strangers and enjoys the process-great.

When the child get older it's pretty much the same rule of thumb. How does he handle the room full of strangers? Does he follow directions and keep a pleasant disposition even when the hours are long and the task boring or uncomfortable? Can she read and memorize lines or do the same blocking over and over? Can he follow directions? Is she inventive and bright and quick? How's the old concentration?

Those questions tell you if the child could do it. The other question is does she want to? And do you want to? That is, once you understand that being the parent of an acting child is a full time job. You must have a car full of gas, an encyclopedic knowledge of Chicagoland geography and nothing else to do. During the school year, auditions for children are held after school. If you live in the suburbs, there goes sitting down to dinner at six.

It's tough to schedule after-school activities and get homework done. The children's wardrobes need constant attention. Is one child acting and the other(s) not? Who will mind them? And how left out of it will they feel? Casting directors really hate it when each child called to audition brings an entourage of six or seven family members who squat in the ever-shrinking waiting room. And do any of you like breaking all existing plans to haul into town for an audition? Pictures, voice-tapes, clothes, answering machines, beepers, car phones, these are not cheap. Got the cash? Want to spend it? Okay.

Okay, I'm warned and we still want to do it. What do I need?

Pretty much what the bigger actors need. (I'd say grown up but in some cases that's vastly inaccurate.)

First of all, the child needs an adult whose job it is to take care of him, his scheduling, wardrobe, finances, pictures, and transportation. This adult also has to be able to realize when the child is pushed too far and needs to take a break, either short term or permanently. This adult must be there for him, not push him. The adult's job is to make acting a possibility, not a chore. It's a rare and remarkable parent who can do this. There are many who succeed, even more who don't.

You need an agent if you are really serious. You can do extra work without one, but extra work has all of the grunt and precious little of the glamour. You may luck into a little non-union commercial by having a relative or neighbor who is casting for a child. Or you may be spotted by a casting director out doing street casting. One job without an agent is okay, but if you are really serious you need a GOOD agent.

How do I find a good agent?

The Act One Reports lists all the union-franchised agents. You want to deal only with legitimate, reputable, franchised agents. There are scumbags out there who prey on parents dreams or greed and will take you to the cleaners. Consult the Act One Reports. The listings will tell you if an agency has a children's department and which agent handles it. The Act One Reports will also tell you whether the agency wishes you to approach them by mail or in person.

What do you want to look out for? The same things apply to children's agencies as adult agencies. No agency should charge you to register or require you to spend big bucks having pictures taken by THEIR photographer. Watch out for the ones who promise the moon, stars and everything else.

How do I approach a professional agent to see if she is interested in my child?

If you are submitting your child to an agency by mail, you do not need professional pictures. School pictures really aren't that good nor are the ones at the local portrait studio. What the agents want is nice clear candid snapshots where the children look like themselves. These should be of the child alone. Simple, decent clothes, not costumes or bathing suits. You can send one that is a close up and one that shows the whole body.

Enclose a cover letter and the vital statistics: name, social security number, telephone number(s) and address. Also include information such as date of birth, hair and eye color, weight, height, sizes, measurements (such as waist and inseam) and the date of the photograph. The more recent the photo the better. You can add the child's talents: languages they speak, musical instruments they play, singing, dancing, special skills, sports, hobbies.

It usually takes several weeks for the agency to get back to you. Someone will call or write to you to schedule an interview. At the interview the agent will get to meet you and the child, see if you understand the business, and see how well the child can read a scene or a commercial and maybe even put her on tape. Although you are a big part of the team, let the agent talk to the child. Don't answer for her, unless, of course, she is pre-verbal.

Instead of submitting by mail, you can also go to the agency on the days they have open registration. Not all agencies do this. I don't recommend this as a practice with small children. The waiting room is crammed with nervous actors, the waits are long and tempers can be short. She will make a less than rosy first impression and, after a long, frustrating wait, may not be on her best behavior. Rejection, should it come, is better for the little one by mail, not face to face in a crowded office after a long wait. Save yourself the aggravation and submit by mail.

What will an agent do?

Just as with older actors, the agent should get your child auditions. The actor gets the work but the agent gets the audition. The same policies and protocols hold true for children as they do for adults. You must have an agent and you and the agent must work well together.

The agent should also make sure that there are enough pictures on file and answer any of your pertinent questions. Children are constantly growing and changing so the agent must advise you about when to get new pictures. While the child is just starting out snapshots will suffice. Eventually you will need professional 8x10s.

The agent will guide you in selecting a photographer and in the types of looks you want. You may also want a composite if your child wants to model. A composite shows many different looks.

The agent may answer questions about appearance. Cut the hair? Get a "flipper" to fill in a missing tooth? She may also advise on classes to take or on the arrangement of a resume. No reputable agent will hard sell you on classes.

What's this I hear about a work permit?

Children under 16 must have a work permit. It must be renewed every year, preferably on the child's birthday. If your child is listed with more than one agent, you need one for each agent representing the child. You need a letter of intent from the agent(s), a form from the child's school signed by the principal, a doctor's certificate and a birth certificate or some other verification of age. Call the Illinois Film Office or the State Board of Education to arrange this.

Keep one copy of the work permit for yourself and return the other to the agent's office. You will need to bring your copy of the work permit to every job.

The agent, once your child is booked on a job, negotiates the contract, getting the best deal possible. The child looks out for and makes sure that the payment is prompt and full.

The chapter on agents will explain more of the procedures, etiquette and division of labor as do the chapters on casting directors and other aspects of the business.

Is there anything different that kids and their parents should know?

The information outlined in the rest of the book is true for kids. In the case of kids it will be the parents and not the actor himself who assume a lot of the responsibilities.

But here are a few kid rules. Don't travel to auditions with the entire family and half of the scout troop. One parent, one kid- okay, maybe the baby too- but that's it.

Parents, bring something to keep the child amused at auditions. And don't grill him and make him tense before he goes into the audition. And don't, for heaven's sake, say as he emerges, "Well, did you get it?"

Also, Mom and Dad, no sugar before the audition. Casting directors hate a roomful of sugar-high, knee-high actors. And allow your child to be a child. I have gagged at the sight of four foot high Madonna wannabes in rhinestones, hot pants and bare midriffs. It reeks of child porn. Just as unattractive are 10 year olds who act like tiny 40 year old Diane Sawyer types.

On the subject of child abuse, and believe me tricking a child out like a sidewalk harlot is just that, I have also seen very small children of five or six dumped at a casting director's office. They were left there while the parent went God knows where. Abandoned. Six o'clock came and no parent. The casting director stayed open until the child was at last collected- BY THE AGENT. You can just bet that poor tyke was called in again soon. The same thing has happened, and by the same parents, at a shoot. Makes you wonder.

What should we watch out for?

Parents, be wary of anyone approaching you or your child and promising a role or work. It may very well be that they are in fact legitimate agents or casting directors, but it may also be that they are scam artists. Ask for a card and follow up. For goodness sake call SAG and AFTRA and the State of Illinois Department of Labor if you are uneasy about the people or company. Beware of anything that comes in the mail, soliciting money or pictures or sending you to an agency. An agent takes 15-20% for print and never more than 10% (usually paid on top by the client) for everything else. Casting directors are NEVER paid by talent!

Can you give a specific example of a scam-like operation?

Modeling schools that claim to also be talent agencies. Not a good idea. It doesn't take a rocket scientist to see that they are out to cash in on your dreams of stardom for little Prunella. There are schools and there are talent agencies. The two should never be confused or combined. If you check the Act One Reports you will find the franchised talent agencies. Stick with those. They are, almost exclusively, in the city, but then so are the casting directors and the ad agencies.

A word of caution about casting directors in Chicago pulling the same kinds of stunts. I would be wary, to say the least, of taking my child to a casting director who pushes his classes on my child. Good casting directors do not foist their classes on children and parents.

One excellent veteran Chicago casting director who teaches on a very limited scale keeps the classes small and on an invitation or agent-recommendation-only-basis. Others are not so ethical. I have heard a casting director-school operator tell parents who brought in children for a film audition that, of course, the school's children always got the first calls and the special attention, the coaching and the hints to win. She said that there were calls only for her students, whether they had agents or not. I would also steer away from any school/casting office operated by parents who have children in the business.

There are some dreadful, opportunistic people out there preying on parents' ambitions, dreams and gullibility. Ask anyone for their credentials, in writing, and then check them out with the unions and the state. The vast majority of agents and casting directors are excellent. It takes only one, however, to sour the dream and do heaven-knows-what harm to your child. REPORT ANY ABUSES TO THE UNIONS AND THE BOARD OF LABOR IMMEDIATELY!

One last word, and I repeat myself I know, but please watch your child and yourself for signs of overload and burnout. This is for fun, maybe for a college fund, but it should not pay the family's way and put untold burdens on the children. Don't set them out to fulfill your dreams, don't live vicariously through them. Do not punish, even subtly, if they do not win the audition. So much goes into the decisions. Keep it light. Keep it fun. And know when to let go. Know when to let them say "enough" or say it for them if they feel that, even though they are miserable, they would be letting you down if they gave up. Above all, let them be children- free, silly and beautiful in whatever way they were made.

PART THREE:

WORKING AT BEING AN ACTOR

WORKING WHEN YOU'RE NOT WORKING

Use the time when you're not working to work. Use the time getting better, not just getting by. USE the time. When to greater or lesser degrees our identities and self-esteem are dependent on what we are doing professionally, the time of doing nothing can make us feel like nothing. But it need not be so. This can be a wonderful time for growth, invention and discovery which can be impossible in the demanding and constrained time of rehearsal and performance.

To be ready to be receptive in this fallow time, we must plow up all the weeds that can sap and choke us. We must first be rid of the old attitude of "I'm nothing if I'm not in a play or film" or "I'm never going to work again." They just get in the way.

So too does rehearsing old grievances and wrongs, real or imagined. The green room at the Globe heard plenty of grousing and sniping, I'm sure. Traditional or no, it's got to GO. It's unhealthy. It does no good, only harm. I don't want to sound too New Age about this, but it does create a very negative atmosphere, feeding your insecurities and reinforcing others' doubts about you. You didn't get the part. Okay. Now get on with your life.

Choose to be positive. Concentrate on the things you've done, can do and will do. Use whatever it takes, from Dale Carnegie to Shakti Gawain, but be positive. Realize there is much to learn and this is a great time for learning, unlearning and relearning. Use the time to get out of the bad habits you've gotten into when you were being overwhelmed and under prepared. Toss out cynicism and recharge wonder. Get excited about acting, not just getting employed.

Employ yourself to work for yourself. Give yourself tasks that will keep you honed and ready when work, or the chance for work, comes.

Learn new pieces now so that you don't fly around panic stricken digging up and halfway preparing speeches and songs just before an audition. Read plays you've heard about or haven't reread for years. Go on safari and stalk the elusive two-minute monologues where they lurk: in libraries, bookstores or friends' collections. While hunting, collect all those biographies, memoirs and treatises on acting and directing you've been meaning to get to. Read them. Read novels and diaries. There are often audition gems to be found there. Or write.

Rent videos that show other time periods or acting styles. Try doing your audition pieces in those or other styles and see what happens. Try the pieces in other voices and dialects. Learn new dialects from tapes or teachers. Learn a new skill or improve an existing one. Get to the gym and get fit. Losing that gut could give you another few years at romantic leads.

Organize a weekly workshop with other actors and directors-but with the no-whining rule strictly enforced. For many years I was part of the Chicago Actors' Workshop. We met weekly to listen to and guide each other's monologues and share areas of expertise. A member trained in improvisation would take several meetings. A member-director would help with cold readings and interview techniques. We worked on stage combat, styles, and dialects. Eventually we developed and produced several showcases. We became a support and survival group. Such a group is easily set up and the benefits are incalculable.

Take time to observe people and do some serious eavesdropping. Collect characters; hoard them away. Take time to look at yourself. Take time just to be quiet. Walking is good. Alone with yourself, you'll discover much that other demands on your time and talent have kept hidden. Additionally, there may be some strange new characters and voices waiting in there. Meet them.

Go to the theatre. Not to cavil or cluck, but to see what's happening. You may see something you might like to "Borrow" - a movement or a moment.

Hint: a schedule, anathema as it may be to many, really is the best plan. Set your goals and set them in a schedule. Demand of yourself one new monologue every two weeks, for instance. Read a Shakespeare play a week. Plan daily workouts and walks. See a play a month. Decide what you can and want to do and then make it happen. With a schedule you'll not wander and piffle away the time. And you'll be less likely to wallow. Needless to say, watch your diet. Fill your days, not your stomach. If you are tempted to chemically insulate yourself remember that whereas you may be altered and anesthetized you also are inhibiting insights and connections, making communication impossible. Get out and get busy. Obviously, this is the time to update pictures and resumes, to make rounds and let people know that you are available again.

Now that you have time and the imperative, prepare for auditions. This is not to say you need not prepare when you are working, you know that. A constant refrain from casting authorities and agents has been the painfully obvious lack of preparation by many actors. This may sound like a broken record to many, but be prepared with pictures for each audition and callback.

Schedule yourself so that you are on time- and be prepared with the agent's number if you even suspect you are going to be late. Pick up sides as soon as they are available and spend serious time becoming familiar with, if not memorizing, the material. Make strong, positive choices. By being in touch with the material, you can really listen and nimbly respond to the director's notes. Then you can concentrate on the requested adjustments, not on frantically remembering lines. We want film and television projects to scout and audition in Chicago. They will as long as we continue to show ourselves professionals. Local directors and casting authorities will continue to call an actor only if she stays up to speed.

Lastly, this less pressured time allows for quiet reflection. It can be a time to examine and reorder priorities, to look back and ahead as well as undistractedly at the present. Is your career headed in the right direction and making the expected progress? Do you still want the same things? Are you going after them the same way and is that way working? Have you outgrown your audition pieces, your pictures, your associations? Is your agent right for you? Is your theatre showcasing you properly? Are you in touch with yourself. Tough questions. Add to them, "What have I learned from my last job, last interview?" These recollections in tranquillity can prove more profitable than many a paycheck.

WORKING WHILE YOU'RE WORKING

Congratulations! Mazel Tov! Well done you! You've got a job-great. You've got it but, obviously, that's only step one. Sure, now you go to rehearsal, learn the lines, build the character and show up every night. But by no means is that all.

A great deal of work has to happen before the first rehearsal. The amount of work you can do depends on how much time you have. Last minute casting doesn't allow for a great deal of preparation.

On the question of being off book by the first rehearsal- that's up to the director. Some appreciate it, what with the limited rehearsal time we are allowed. Some however are set against it. Ask. If you run into the "don't learn them till rehearsal," that doesn't mean you park the script under the potted geraniums and don't pick it up again until you're on your way to the first rehearsal. Read and re-read it. Take notes and record anything that occurs to you.

Patrick Tucker, the British director, is fond of this technique and advocates at least six reads during which time he records all his thoughts- especially the 'silly' ones. Write down any questions and look up any unfamiliar words or phrases or references. Get translations of foreign words. This is vitally important not only to know what you are saying (of no small importance) but also to encounter such a problem and not solve it is tantamount to placing a full page ad in Variety saying I am one lazy actor.

Sometimes you may come across a word for which you know the meaning and usual usage but which strikes you as odd in this context. It may be a regional usage which will give you a clue about your character. If you are working with a British play or a British translation, the word in question may be in a usage peculiar to England. England and America are, after all, two countries separated by a common language. There are English/American dictionaries. Or consult your local Anglophile.

If you are to be off book (or in that neighborhood) and after you have reread and made notes, make a tape recording of your lines. Put the tape into a Walkman-like device and wear it around the house whilst doing idiot chores. Mindless work, like dishes or laundry, is perfect for subconscious planting. This way the usually mind-numbing tedium can be profitable. Put the headphones on when you go for your walk. You'll clear your head in the fresh air and pound in the lines, saving you invaluable rehearsal time.

If you need to be in shape, as in having to do a lot or wear a little, get to the gym or to class. Don't leave it until the end of a long rehearsal day. And who knows, getting in shape may take longer than you'd anticipated. If you need to sing, get your voice in shape. If you are playing an instrument, practice. If you need a dialect, find out from your director exactly what is required and get busy with tapes or a coach.

Actresses (or in some cases, actors): if you are going to be stuffed into corsets or high heels, practice. Both can be nasty surprises to your spine and concentration.

When you have completed your list of questions, call the director and arrange to meet before rehearsals begin. There will be more time now, and fewer demands and distractions, than later.

Before rehearsals begin is the time to do your research. Presumably you are not playing yourself. There will be insights and experiences needed that are outside your own history. Decide what you need to learn and go find it. Be inventive. Perpetually busy actor Gerry Becker, who does extensive research, offers these ideas: "To get real life experiences I physically go to the places and talk to the people whenever possible. For *One For The Road* in which I played a torturer/interrogator, I spent as much time with cops as possible. I talked to them individually and just hung out. Additionally, the character was ultra right wing and thought he was the voice of God. That was the central spin on him. I went daily to very right wing churches. I spent two months talking to former political prisoners from Chile. You have to go into these experiences without any judgments or preconceptions. For the *Howard Beach Story* in which I played a lawyer, I spent a week with the State's Attorney's office. For *The Normal Heart* and *Puppetmaster* I went to synagogue. And for *Puppetmaster* I watched and read everything I could about the Holocaust. Conversely for *Hotel Paradise*, I studied old Peter Sellers films. I like to work this way. It's like detective work. In the end you use maybe two things out of ten, you cannot be limited by the research."

Once rehearsals begin, be ready. Be ready to listen and make notes and adjustments. I repeat, be ready to listen. It sounds simple, simplistic, even simple minded but often we are too busy to listen to the director, the stage manager, other actors, ourselves. Organize your life so that you can arrive at rehearsal ready and so that you can come home afterwards and pound in the day's work. During rehearsal, work is not limited to rehearsal hours. Be careful of your time and energy. Direct them and your concentration where needed, which is not necessarily the green room or lunch table. Of course, relax and unwind and schmooze but don't lose your priorities.

The same advice holds for the run of the show. I have seen (and perhaps given) dressing room performances that surpassed anything on stage. Schedule your day around performances. Get rest, exercise and good nutrition. (Yes, Mom.) Watch what you ingest, and by this I don't mean just alcohol and other drugs which will play havoc with performances and careers. Caffeine and sugar can muck about with your energy. Have everything ready at the theatre so you're not throwing things around at fifteen minutes searching for your eye liner. Check your props. And take as long as you need to get ready to go on just as long as you're ready at your cue. You cannot just put down a crossword puzzle and make an entrance.

All too soon the show will close. It is a natural fact that weeks, months, years later you will be stopped short one day with a revelation of, "Oh, that's what that line meant; that's how I should have moved." Perhaps, if the gods are kind, you'll get another crack at the role. Painful as these posthumous revelations can be, they are nothing compared to the souls-in-torment brand of agony prompted by knowing that you wasted time and energy, robbing your performance and cheating your audience and yourself. To prevent this, get ready. The readiness is all.

GLOSSARY

AEA- Actors' Equity Association, usually referred to as Equity. The union which represents stage actors.

AFTRA- American Federation of TV and Radio Artists, the union for TV and radio performers.

Actors' night- A night or nights set aside by a theatre on which actors can attend the performance for free.

Agent- The person who represents the actor (talent). He or she arranges auditions, handles bookings and negotiates rates and collects a commission for doing so.

Availability- Is the actor available on the day of the call-back or shoot.

Bite and smile- The term used for commercials (usually for food products) in which the actor does just that: takes a bite of the product and then smiles to register how delicious it is.

Booking- A job.

Booking out- Calling your agent to say that you will be unavailable for a period of time either because you are working, will be out of town or otherwise engaged.

Breakdown- The list of characters needed for a film or commercial and a brief description of each.

Buy-out- When the actor is paid a set fee for doing a commercial in lieu of residuals.

Callback- Being asked to return for a second or third audition.

Casting Director- The person called by the producer to arrange auditions and aid in the casting of a film, commercial or production. The casting director calls the agent, who in turn calls the actor.

CAT- Chicago Area Theatres. One of the contracts under which Chicago Equity theatres work.

Cattlecall- A huge audition to which most of the immediate city has been called.

Check avail- Term used when a casting director calls the actor's agent to see if the actor is available on the day of a shoot. It is not a booking but it says that the actor is being seriously considered for the job.

Check-in- Calling an agent to inquire about work or to let her know what you are up to.

Commission- The money an actor pays to the agent for securing work. Agents may take no more than 10% for union work, unless it's print where the rates are 15-20%.

Comps- Complimentary tickets. Free tickets are given to Professionals to attend plays.

Composite- A single sheet of several different poses used by actors looking for modeling work.

Conflict- Does the actor have a commercial currently running for this sponsor's competitor and/or is the actor already committed elsewhere on the date(s) of the shoot?

Conflict sheet- The piece of paper at an audition which asks that the actor state whether he has a conflict with the product and/ or the shoot dates.

Copy- The words you speak in a commercial.

Cover letter- The letter which accompanies the actor's picture and resume when he sends it out to agents and casting directors.

Demo- A commercial that is made to test a product or the commercial itself. A demonstration. A trial run. Actors are paid at a different rate for demos than for actual commercials.

Demo tape- An approximately two-and-one-half-minute voice-over tape which actors and agent use to solicit work. The tape gives examples of the actor's range.

Eligible Performer- A non-Equity actor who is allowed to attend Equity auditions because he has either accumulated enough Equity hours in the EMC program or has made the union scale wage for a set amount of time and can be considered a "professional" actor. Eligible performers must obtain identification cards from Equity.

EMC- Equity Membership Candidate. An actor who is accruing hours towards joining Equity.

Exclusive- Represented by one agent only. The actor may only take auditions/bookings through that one agent.

Extra- Background, or atmosphere actors in a film or commercial.

Freelance- Another term for working with several agents as opposed to be represented exclusively by only one.

Generals- The day or days of auditions which theatres and casting directors set aside annually for seeing new actors. Actors schedule appointments and, at the allotted time, perform one or two monologues.

Headshot- The 8x10 photograph of an actor. Usually just his head and shoulders. Three quarter (3/4) body shots are also used and fall under the generic term headshot.

Hotline- The recorded messages listing information of upcoming auditions.

Iced- An actor is asked to keep the day of a shoot open, but is not officially booked yet.

Industrial- A film that teaches. Used by companies to train employees or for other educational purposes. They are not for broadcast or public performance.

Look- What the actor is supposed to look like for the audition- nice casual, upscale, blue collar, corporate, etc.

Look-see- When an actor is sent to a photographer's studio for a possible job. A Polaroid is taken.

LORT- League of Regional Theatres. One of the types of Equity contacts used in Chicago and elsewhere.

Mark- The spot on the floor on which the actor must stand to be in frame for the camera. Usually used as "Find your mark" or "Hit your mark."

Multi-listed- Being represented by more than one agent for auditions. The opposite of being exclusive.

Must join/Must pay- An actor who has done his first union commercial under a Taft Hartley is a must join after 30 days.

Narrator- The person either on- or off-camera who talks directly to the audience. Narration is paid at a different rate than day player.

Narration- Voice-over work that is not a commercial. Usually industrial or educational.

National- A commercial, either voice-over or on-camera, which airs all across the country. These commercials yield substantial residuals.

O/C- On-camera. Usually applies to commercial and industrial work. The opposite of V/O (voice-over).

Open registration- The day or portion of a day on which actors may come to a talent agency without an appointment to register.

Overtime- The same as in any occupation. The unions regulate how many hours the actors may work. After that period, the actors are paid overtime. If the sessions goes long enough this can become double overtime and golden overtime. Serious money can be made here. Keep track of your hours - report them.

Pilot- The first or trial episode of a proposed series.

Pilot season- The several months during which pilots are cast in Los Angeles. Some Chicago actors go out to California for this period.

Point of purchase- An industrial-like film shown in stores to demonstrate a new product.

Prepared piece- A monologue which the actor himself selects and presents for an audition. The opposite of reading from the script.

Principal- The major character in a commercial or film. The opposite of extra.

Print- Photographic modeling.

Proofsheet- The sheets of photographs a photographer gives the actor. All the shots are reproduced in miniature. The actor (and agent) uses the proofsheet to select the pictures she wants to be blown up and used as headshots.

Pull- When agents, at the request of a casting director, pull pictures of actors from the files for a submission.

Reel- A videotape of scenes featuring an actor. On-camera actors and their agents use this to solicit work.

Regional- a commercial, either voice-over or on-camera, which runs only in certain markets.

Request- When a casting director or her client makes a request for a specific actor.

Residual- The moneys paid actors for the rebroadcast of their work- either commercials or theatrical film.

Resume- The actor's credits and training along with other vital information. It is printed, cut to fit the 8x10 headshot and attached to the headshot with staples or glue. It must be up to date.

SAG- Screen Actors' Guild. The union which represents actors when they appear on film.

Scale- The minimum salary required by the union for an actor to work under a specific contract.

Sides- The scene(s) or pages of script which an actor is expected to prepare for an audition.

Sign-in- The sheet(s) at an audition which the actor fills in with information.

Slate- Giving your name and sometimes the name of your agent at the beginning of your audition, either voice-over or on-camera.

Storyboard- The cartoon-like display of what happens in a commercial.

Submission- When an actor sends his headshot and resume to an agent or casting director to be considered for work. Likewise, when an agent sends pictures and resumes of her clients to a casting director.

Survival job (or 'day job')- Employment, often temp work or waiting tables, which actors take to pay the bills between acting jobs.

Taft-Hartley- The agreement with the labor union through which an actor may do his first union job without having to join the union.

Talent- the generic term for actors.

Theatre release- The time at which you must be released from a shoot in order for you to be at the theatre in time to perform.

Up-grade- When an actor is booked as an extra for a shoot and then is given principal status.

V/O- Voice-over. The unseen-but-heard actor.